SNOWSHOE ROUTES

washington

SNOWSHOE ROUTES
washington

DAN A. NELSON

THE
MOUNTAINEERS

Published by
The Mountaineers
1001 SW Klickitat Way, Suite 201
Seattle, WA 98134

First edition, 1998

Published simultaneously in Great Britain by Cordee, 3a DeMontfort
Street, Leicester, England, LE1 7HD

Manufactured in the United States of America

Edited by Paula Thurman
Maps by Jerry Painter
All photographs by the author unless otherwise noted.
Cover design by Elizabeth Watson
Book design by Alice Merrill
Book layout by Green Rhino Graphics

Cover photograph: Pat O'Hara/Corbis
Frontispiece: On the trail below Cathedral Peak.

Nelson, Dan A.
    Snowshoe routes, Washington / Dan A. Nelson. -- 1st ed.
        p.   cm.
    ISBN 0-89886-585-9
    1. Snowshoes and snowshoeing--Washington (State)--Guidebooks.
2. Trails--Washington (State)--Guidebooks.   3. Washington (State)-
-Guidebooks.   I. Title.
    GV853.N45   1998
    796.9'2'09797--dc21
                                                        98-22546
                                                            CIP

Contents

Preface • 9

Introduction • 13

1. Hurricane Hill • 29
2. Mount Angeles/Heather Park • 31
3. Eagle Point • 33
4. Mount Townsend • 35
5. Lena Lake/Valley of Silent Men • 37
6. Coat Pass • 40
7. Coleman Glacier • 42
8. White Salmon Creek • 45
9. Artist Point • 48
10. Middle Fork Nooksack • 50
11. Schriebers Meadow • 53
12. Sauk Mountain • 56
13. Iron Mountain • 59
14. Segelsen Ridge • 61
15. Rat Trap Pass • 64
16. Crystal Lake • 67
17. Kennedy Hot Springs • 69
18. Mount Pilchuck • 73
19. Heather Lake • 75
20. Lake 22 • 78
21. Boardman Lake • 80
22. Bear Lake • 84
23. Mallardy Ridge • 86
24. Kelcema Lake • 87
25. Marten Creek • 90
26. Big Four Ice Caves Viewpoint • 92
27. Coal Creek • 94

28. Silver Star View • 96
29. Upper River Run • 99
30. Cedar Falls • 102
31. Paul Mountain • 104
32. Buck Mountain • 107
33. Lookout Mountain • 110
34. Eagle Creek • 112
35. East Fork Foss River • 115
36. Tonga Ridge • 117
37. Lake Susan Jane • 120
38. Skyline Lake • 123
39. Lake Valhalla • 125
40. Surprise Lake • 128
41. Lanham Lake • 130
42. Wenatchee Ridge • 132
43. Chiwaukum Creek • 134
44. Eight-mile Creek • 137
45. Talapus Lake • 139
46. Source Lake • 141
47. Commonwealth Basin • 144
48. Kendall Peak Lakes • 146
49. Lower Gold Creek Basin • 148
50. Mount Margaret • 150
51. Keechelus Ridge • 153
52. Amabilis Mountain • 156
53. Thorp Mountain • 159
54. Hex Mountain • 161
55. Sasse Ridge • 164
56. Salmon la Sac Creek • 167
57. Cooper River • 169
58. Indian Creek • 171
59. Sun Top • 174
60. Bullion Basin • 177
61. Mowich Lake • 179
62. Paul Peak • 182
63. Mount Beljica • 184
64. Kautz Creek • 187
65. Eagle and Chutla Peaks Trail • 190
66. Rampart Ridge • 191
67. Wonderland Trail • 194

68. Reflection and Louise Lakes • 196
69. Pinnacle Saddle • 199
70. Mazama Ridge • 201
71. Panorama Point • 203
72. Silver Falls/Grove of the Patriarchs • 206
73. Olallie Creek • 209
74. Packwood Lake • 211
75. Sand Lake • 213
76. Cramer Lake • 215
77. Goat Peak • 217
78. Mount St. Helens Summit • 219
79. June Lake • 221
80. Worm Flows • 223
81. Table Rock/Squaw Peak • 226
Appendix: Addresses and Telephone Numbers • 231
Index • 235

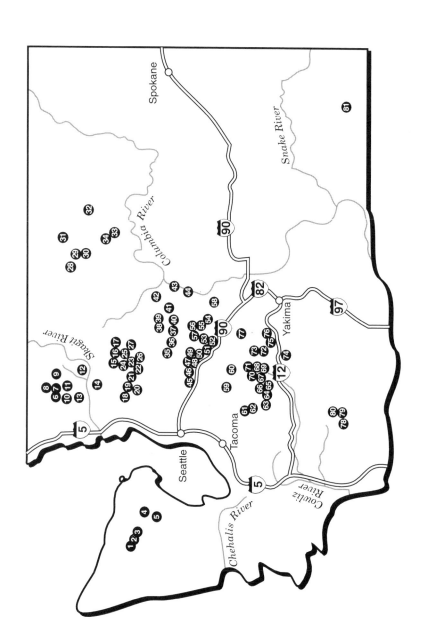

Preface

The tremendous popularity of hiking in the Pacific Northwest is one of the reasons for the remarkable growth of recreational snowshoeing. Summer hikers are loath to give up their favorite pastime simply because the seasons change.

So, come winter, hikers have two options—step onto a pair of cross-country skis, or strap on snowshoes. For the past few decades, skis have been the preferred choice for backcountry enthusiasts. But not everyone wants to take the time, or make the considerable effort, needed to master the art of cross-country skiing in mountain country. Snowshoeing has become a popular alternative.

Since 1990, the number of people enjoying a winter hike on snowshoes has increased by 300 percent. Probably the main reason for this trend is the ease with which beginners can become accomplished snowshoers. Anyone who knows how to walk, knows how to use snowshoes—just strap them on and walk, it's as simple as that. Another reason snowshoes are increasingly popular is that hikers can get to the same areas in winter that they hike to in summer. They can move easily through thick forests and up steep slopes. Skis, on the other hand, are more difficult to maneuver on forest trails, and uphill slopes pose tougher challenges for novice skiers. (Although the downhill run is undeniably more fun on skis.)

The biggest drawback for snowshoers to date has been the lack of information on destinations. Sure, hikers can travel many of the same trails on snowshoes that they can in the summer, but more often than not, the trailheads for those trails are inaccessible by car. Fortunately, the surge in interest in cross-country skiing in the 1970s prompted the state of Washington to build and maintain a series of Sno-Parks throughout the state. These facilities are merely parking lots that are kept cleared of snow and access roads that are kept plowed during the winter. More than 110

The distinctive towers known as the Needles are visible from the Silver Star route

Sno-Parks are maintained for winter recreationists, with no less than 50 devoted solely to nonmotorized recreationists.

Cross-country skiers and snowmobilers have utilized these Sno-Parks for two decades now. Many of the facilities also feature groomed ski trails, groomed snowmobile trails, and a few even have tracks set for skiers who prefer that mode of skiing.

While the skinny skis and screaming snowmobiles crowd the groomed roads and wide trails leading out of these parking areas, snowshoers can take advantage of the solitude found on the forest trails that angle away from the roads. These snow-laden paths are impossible—if not illegal—for snowmobilers to negotiate and too difficult for the majority of skiers to attempt. But a hiker wearing a pair of modern snowshoes can climb the snowy trail as easily as a hiker can trudge up switchbacks in summer. In fact, snowshoers have a decided advantage over their summer colleagues simply because they can often walk right over the top of many difficult obstacles—thick brush, fallen logs, treacherous talus fields, and so forth. A heavy blanket of snow can level the most difficult field so that in winter, hikers feel like they are hiking through an open meadow, whereas in summer, hikers may find the same area to be an impassable slope of slide alder.

Unfortunately, that blanket of snow also makes finding a specific trail next to impossible sometimes. That's where this book comes in. I've put together 81 of my favorite winter hikes around Washington and present them here as a means of helping other hikers find the beauty of the winter backcountry without the hassle of trying to pick and choose a route. Of course, the routes I describe here are not as easy to follow as a snow-free summer trail, nor should snowshoers think they have to follow my exact footprints. Part of the mystique and wonder of snowshoe hiking is the ability to explore anywhere—a route is limited only by a snowshoer's physical and mental limits, tempered with a heavy dose of common sense and avalanche awareness.

Line of stubby trees coated with rime ice

Winter meadow near June Lake

Introduction

Snowshoes are the earliest known means of making travel on snow easier. The best archeological evidence suggests these early "foot-extenders" originated in Central Asia about 4000 B.C. Further evidence shows that without this mode of winter transportation, aboriginal people would not have been able to journey to what is now North America via the Bering Strait.

Snowshoes are a natural for modern-day winter trekking, as more and more people are coming to realize. With a little planning and preparation, you can embrace the beauties of the backcountry year-round.

Definite benefits are derived by supplementing warm-weather hiking with snowshoeing come winter. In addition to the readily apparent payoffs of summer hiking—escape from the mechanized, hectic world, if only for a short time; strenuous, healthy workouts in beautiful surroundings; the thrill of accomplishment after hiking a long trail or climbing a steep peak; communion with the natural world—winter wilderness rambling offers its own rewards. The landscape is more serene, covered in a sound-absorbing carpet of snow. No irritating swarms of bugs gnaw on your exposed skin, and far fewer humans compete for a spot in the quiet wilderness.

Of course, there are other winter recreation considerations, most notably the weather. The cold weather. This factor influences all the benefits—and dangers—of exploring a snow-shrouded wilderness.

The lower temperatures of winter make snow recreation more intense than its warmer-season counterparts. The planning and preparation of a trip takes more time and thought. More equipment and clothing are needed for winter camping. The discomforts of a poorly planned trip are more acute. But the pleasures of a good outing are more profound.

STEPPING OUT INTO THE SNOW

The most visible change from summer to winter is your method of locomotion. When the snow flies, it is no longer possible to merely lace up your sturdy boots and head up the trail—try doing that after a deep pack of Cascade concrete has filtered down on the hills, and you'll find yourself exhausted in the first 100 yards. That's where snowshoes come in. Snowshoes are the easiest way to get acquainted with winter wilderness. The basics of snowshoeing are simple—it's just like walking, but with bigger feet. Of course, there is a bit more to it than that, but essentially, any other techniques are simply variations of other walking strides.

Snowshoes themselves come in a variety of forms. Traditional shoes are made with wooden frames and rawhide laces for decking. These range in shape from round "bearpaws" to long, tapered "Yukons," which feature lots of surface area and extended tails that drag in the snow to help keep the shoes pointed forward. You can still find wooden shoes, although the lace decking is usually made with strips of neoprene rubber these days, but the best bet for any general-use winter hiking is the "modern" design. This is essentially a narrow "bearpaw." It features an aluminum or rigid plastic oval frame with a solid decking of synthetic fabric. Several shoes are now available that are made from extruded plastic. Some of these solid plastic shoes are lightweight, affordable, and for the most part, very effective. Regardless of the type, make sure the shoes have ice spikes—called crampons, or cleats—under the forefoot and heel plates.

The size of your snowshoes depends on a number of factors, primarily your weight (including the weight of your pack) and the kind of snow in which you'll be trekking. In the Cascades, the general rule is to plan on heavy, wet snow. Most people under 180 pounds can wear snowshoes in the 8- by 25-inch category. Larger folks, or hikers who will be carrying heavy packs, should consider shoes in the 9- by 30-inch range. Big guys with very heavy packs can go up to a 9- by 36-inch shoe.

If you plan to snowshoe in the Rocky Mountains, or in areas where the snow is generally lighter and fluffier, you'll need to move up a step in shoe size. Before buying a pair of snowshoes, it is a good idea to rent several different pairs to get a feel for which model you prefer and which size is best for you.

FOOTWEAR

Unlike cross-country skiing, there are no specific boots that must be worn with snowshoes. Regular hiking boots, mountaineering boots, "pac" boots, or even cross-country ski boots can be worn with the easy-to-use bindings found on most quality snowshoes. Ideally, you want boots that provide the type of ankle and foot support found in regular hiking boots, but which also keep your feet warm and dry.

Many hiking boot companies have begun to work with snowshoe

makers to design insulated hiking boots specifically for snowshoe trekking. The best option now is to use all-leather hiking boots that are large enough to comfortably allow you to wear a thick layer or two of insulated socks, and then cover the boots with waterproof gaiters. Just don't pack too much wool into your boots, because too tight of a fit will make your feet feel even colder than if there was no insulation.

CLOTHING

In addition to snowshoes, you'll need to carry several layers of bulky clothing in your pack for winter excursions. Avoid anything made with cotton. Instead, you'll need multiple layers of synthetic or wool clothing.

By layering your clothing, you can easily make adjustments when you start to heat up (and you will heat up, as walking in snowshoes is a better aerobic workout than walking on a dry trail) or cool down—just add or subtract a layer or two. Working from the skin out, start with a good base layer of silk or synthetic (polypropylene, Capilene, Thermastat, etc.) long johns. These will form a thin insulating layer next to your skin, but more importantly, they will pull moisture away from your body. Without that "wicking" action, the moisture could end up freezing on your skin, causing almost instant hypothermia.

Over the base layer, add a thin insulating layer, like a wool or synthetic fleece sweater and pants. On very cold days, or if you generally get cold easily, cover this layer with a thicker insulating layer—a fleece jacket or vest. When the wind is blowing or moisture is in the air, top off the whole outfit with a sturdy waterproof parka and pants. This layer will cut the wind and prevent any external water from soaking through.

The idea behind building an insulation "shell" in layers is that you can then easily adjust your clothing to the hiking conditions. When getting started each day, take into consideration not only the weather but also the type of snowshoeing you'll be doing. A lot of climbing early on means you'll be working hard, and if you have too many layers, you'll quickly work up a sweat. To avoid that, adjust the layers to the point where you can just feel a chill as you start out, knowing that within a few steps you'll be warmed up enough to be comfortable, but not overheated.

OTHER GEAR

Every time you venture more than a few yards away from the road on a snowshoe outing, you should be prepared to spend the night under the stars (or under the clouds, as may be more likely). Winter storms can whip up in a hurry, catching you by surprise. What was an easy-to-follow trail during a calm, clear day can disappear into a confusing world of white in a wind-swept snowstorm. Therefore, every member of the party should have a pack loaded with The Mountaineers' Ten Essentials, as well as a few other items that aren't necessarily essential but are good to have on hand in a winter emergency.

The Ten Essentials

1. Extra clothing. This means more clothing than you would wear during the worst weather of the planned outing. If you get injured or lost, you won't be moving around generating heat, so you'll need to be able to bundle up. (See Clothing section.)

2. Extra food. Pack enough so that you'll have leftovers after an uneventful trip. (Those leftovers will keep you fed and fueled during an emergency.)

3. Sunglasses. While necessary for most high-alpine travel, they are absolutely essential for snow. Snow blindness (sunburn of the eyes) can render you immobile and helpless.

4. Knife. There are a multitude of uses; some come easily to mind (whittling kindling for a fire; first-aid applications) while others won't become apparent until you find you don't have a knife handy. A multitool is an even better option because the pliers can be used to repair damaged snowshoes.

5. First-aid kit. Nothing elaborate is needed—especially if you are unfamiliar with some of the uses. Make sure you have adhesive bandages, gauze bandages, pain-relief medicine, etc. A Red Cross first-aid training course is recommended.

6. Fire starter. An emergency campfire provides warmth, but it also has a calming effect on most people. Without it, the night is cold, dark, and intimidating. With it, the night is held at arm's length. A candle or tube of fire-starting ribbon is essential for starting a fire with wet wood.

7. Matches. You can't start a fire without them. Pack in a waterproof container and/or buy the waterproof/windproof variety. Book matches are useless in wind or wet weather, and disposable lighters are unreliable.

8. Flashlight. If caught after dark, you'll need it to follow the trail. If forced to spend the night, you'll need it to set up emergency camp, gather wood, etc. Carry extra batteries and bulb.

9. Map. Carry a topographic map of the area you plan to be in, and know how to read it.

10. Compass. Again, make sure you know how to use it.

In addition to these essentials, I add two small kit bags. One is a repair kit, containing a 20-foot length of nylon cord, a small roll of duct tape, some

1-inch webbing and extra webbing buckles (to replace any that might break on the snowshoe bindings), and a small tube of fast-bonding glue. The other tiny package at the bottom of my pack is my emergency survival kit, which holds a small metal mirror, an emergency Mylar "blanket," a plastic whistle, and a tiny signal smoke canister—all useful for signaling to search groups, whether they are on the ground or in the air.

Other items you might want to carry with you on your snowshoe outings include a small compactible snow shovel and ice saw. Both tools are extremely useful when setting up a camp in the snow. Many snowshoers find ski poles very helpful, especially when climbing or descending hills, and some campers prefer to pull their gear on a sled rather than pack it on their backs.

SNOWSHOEING TECHNIQUE

As I stated at the outset, if you can walk, you can walk on snowshoes. Generally, that is true; however, a few special techniques can help in tricky situations. Heading up and down hills, for instance, can be a problem unless you alter your hiking technique to accommodate the snowshoes.

To climb a hill, kick your toe into the hillside to dig the forefoot cleats into the snow, and then step down, putting weight on the toe so that the cleats get a good, solid bite into the slope. To go back down the hill, lean forward slightly and plant your whole foot solidly on the surface of the snow. This engages the entire surface of the snowshoe on the slope, and by leaning forward, you distribute your weight evenly on all the cleats. If, however, you lean back and keep your weight more on your heels (as you generally would do when hiking), you'll disengage the cleats on the front half of the snowshoe and slide forward.

Also, if you find you need to back up, the first thing you'll notice is the back of the snowshoe drags under your foot and trips you up. Counter this by using your trekking poles to push down on the front of the snowshoe, forcing the back to lift as you lift your foot. This is also the easiest way to turn around on snowshoes.

Perhaps the biggest difference between walking and walking on snowshoes is the distance between your feet. With snowshoes, you'll need to walk a bit straddle-legged so that the shoes don't overlap or hit your legs as you stride.

CAMPING

There is nothing like spending a night in a snowy wilderness setting. The cold, clear sky and quiet forest are unlike anything you'll experience in the summer. But winter camping has different requirements than camping in the other three seasons. In terms of gear, you'll need a cold-weather sleeping bag (something rated to zero degrees at least, or an insulation liner for your three-season bag) and a four-season tent. Here in the wet Northwest, the best bet for sleeping bags are those with synthetic fill, or insulation layers. Synthetic fills are (relatively) inexpensive, work even when wet, and have evolved to be nearly as efficient and compressible as goose down. Goose down is a wonderful insulator and compresses well to fit into a stuffed backpack, but if it gets wet, it is no good at all. Down is also expensive, and if you add a waterproof shell to a down bag (a necessity in Washington's climate), you drive the price through the roof.

For shelter, you can build snow caves, stay in backcountry huts (found on some maintained ski-trail networks), or pitch a tent. The tent is the best option, but it must be sturdy enough to withstand potentially violent winter winds and heavy snowfall. Most backpacking tents are sold as three-season tents and don't have the stability needed to stand up to the extreme abuses of winter. Four-season tents are built sturdier, with more poles, steeper walls (to shed snow), and heavier flies. All that extra engineering is necessary to make them snow-safe, but it also drives up their price. Fortunately, four-season tents can be rented, so you won't have to invest in a new fabric home if you camp only a few times a year.

When setting out on a winter backpacking trip, keep in mind the short daylight hours of winter and the longer amount of time you will need to set up camp. Plan carefully, and err on the side of caution—it's better to cut a trip short than to push on to a planned destination after darkness has fallen.

Setting up a winter camp is much different than doing it in summer. You'll want to do it when you still have plenty of daylight! Remember that the cold weather will slow you down, and you will be setting up your tent wearing mittens or gloves. But before the tent goes up, clear a place for it. Brush off loose snow and/or stomp down a flat pad for the tent floor. If time allows, build a "wind wall" on the windward side of the tent. Do this by packing snow into a thick, semicircular wall up to 4 feet high. This wall deflects the worst of the night's wind around the tent, keeping it warmer and more secure.

While you are setting up camp, "make" water by melting snow. This can take a long time (and burn a lot of stove fuel, so pack extra).

Once your basic camp is set up, if you still have daylight left, you can spiff up the place by building a "kitchen." Excavate a trough roughly 2 feet wide and 2 feet deep. Cut seats into one wall of the trough and a "table" into the other. Step into the trough, and you can then sit down to do your cooking and eating.

Snow blankets the bed of the Methow River

Snow bends a small tree nearly to the ground

BE PREPARED

Winter recreation has some risks inherent to the season. Cold temperatures and wet conditions are the obvious ones, and proper clothing and preparation are essential to help you deal with the cold and wet. But as harsh as the weather conditions can be, it's the snow that poses one of the biggest threats to winter recreationists, especially in the mountains. The danger of avalanche is found anywhere there is a slope with snow on it. Sometimes the danger is minimal, sometimes a slide is inevitable, and frequently you won't be able to tell the difference by looking at the hillside. Knowledge of current snow conditions, recent weather patterns, and future weather forecasts are all necessary to help you understand and evaluate the avalanche danger on a given day, in a given area.

One of the best resources available to winter recreationists is the Northwest Avalanche Center, which keeps detailed records on weather and snow patterns and conditions and makes its findings available to the public via a recorded message line. Every time you plan to venture out into the snowy mountains, you should first dial the Avalanche Center, (206) 526-6677, to get the avalanche danger report for your area of interest. Or failing that, purchase and use a weather radio. These radios tune in special FM frequencies not normally found on home radios. These frequencies, 162.4 to 162.55 megahertz, are reserved for use by the National Oceanic and Atmospheric

Administration (NOAA), so they can broadcast ongoing weather reports and conditions. Frequent mountain weather reports, which include avalanche condition reports, are broadcast on the northwest weather radio.

In addition, you should learn to recognize the clues of avalanche danger. All avalanches start with unstable snow—snow that isn't bonded to the hillside. Avalanches are of two primary types: slab avalanches occur when large solid sections of snow break away at once, and loose snow avalanches occur when unattached snow crystals slide down a slope, dislodging more and more snow as they go.

A quick study of the slope ahead of you can reveal clues to avalanche potential. First, estimate the steepness of the slope. Avalanches are most common on a slope of 30 to 45 degrees, but they can and do release on slopes as gentle as 25 degrees or as steep as 65 or more degrees. Second, take note of the profile of the slope. A slope with a convex profile—that is, it bulges out a bit—is more likely to slide than a concave slope. Third, look at the exposure of the slope. A north-facing slope may be slower to stabilize than other slopes because it doesn't receive as much direct sunlight, and therefore the snow doesn't settle and compact as quickly. A leeward slope tends to become wind-loaded with unstable snow more often than a windward slope, since a windward slope generally has less snow, and what is there is more compacted by the wind.

Wind is a major contributor to avalanche hazards, and the higher and more prolonged the wind, the greater the threat of avalanche.

Other visible clues to avalanche danger include the following:

• Sticky snow, which indicates the surface snow is warmer than the snow below.

• Evidence of recent avalanches. If you see a slope that has apparently slid in the last 24 hours or so, consider it a good indication that snow conditions are unstable.

• Hollow drumming or "whomping" sounds coming from the snow underfoot indicate slab conditions, and a high potential for release.

• Rime ice on trees. This build-up of ice and frost suggests there were high winds during a recent storm, and therefore chances are good that leeward slopes are highly wind-loaded and likely to slide.

• Broken limbs and/or snow plastered to the uphill side of trees shows past avalanche occurrence. A slope that slides once will slide again after the next storm.

Understanding and recognizing these signs isn't all there is to know about avoiding avalanche danger. This discussion simply serves as a brief primer on the subject. More detailed information is readily available in a number of excellent books, including *The ABCs of Avalanche Safety* by E. R. LaChapelle (The Mountaineers Books, 1985).

FINDING A DESTINATION

This book details 81 winter hiking routes in Washington. That is by no stretch a complete inventory of the possible snowshoe outing destinations. The goal of this book is to show some of the better areas to explore and to encourage backcountry enthusiasts to get out in the cold months and enjoy the beauty of the snowbound mountains.

There are hundreds, if not thousands, of hikes available for snowshoe trekkers in this state. The best way to find them is to utilize your library of hiking guide books, your inventory of topographic maps, and your growing knowledge of what makes a good winter hike. Plan a snowshoe hike using these tools, as well as current information on snow and weather conditions.

If you are new to snowshoe hiking, start slow. Pick a short hike for your first outing to get a feel for the sport and your abilities. And above all, be flexible. You may find a hike in these pages that sounds like a perfect outing for you. But if the weather is unfavorable, or avalanche dangers are high in that region, make another choice. You can always hike your first choice another time. Better to explore a hike in a different location than to risk getting caught in an avalanche's path.

Gray jay in tree

Exercise good judgment and basic common sense, take advantage of the knowledgeable rangers and avalanche forecasters, and learn to evaluate avalanche potentials and determine snow conditions and you will have a good outing. Like all outdoor adventures, winter hiking has its dangers, but planning and precaution can mitigate most of them. Be prepared, and you will be safe.

SNO-PARKS

Most of the hikes in this book originate from state Sno-Parks. These facilities are parking areas maintained throughout the winter exclusively for winter recreationists. Many are open for multi-use by skiers, snowmobilers, dog mushers, snowshoers, and sledders, although nearly half are set aside for nonmotorized sports. Even if a Sno-Park is open to snowmobilers, there is no reason to pass it by. Typically, snowmobilers will stick to the groomed roads and trails leading away from the Sno-Park, leaving plenty of untracked areas for snowshoers to explore.

Permits are required to park in these facilities, and the permit fees are used to keep parking spaces plowed, bathrooms clean and maintained, and ski and snowmobile trails groomed and maintained. Washington State Sno-Park permits are available by the day, by the week, or for an entire season, and thanks to a cooperative recreation program, the Washington permit is also accepted in Oregon and Idaho. (And permits from those states are accepted here.)

USING THIS BOOK

The route descriptions in this guide are self-explanatory. But keep a few things in mind as you browse through the book, looking for that perfect outing.

Rating the Trails

The rating system for the hikes is subjective, and not everyone will agree with every rating. The individual ratings are based on the following guidelines:

Easiest: No previous snowshoe experience is required. These are great trails for first-timers who want to get a feel for the sport. Generally, elevation gain and loss is small and avalanche dangers are minimal at all times. These are good routes for groups with children or when campers are pulling loads of gear on sleds.

More difficult: A bit more climbing is required as these trails feature more elevation gain. Some previous snowshoe experience is helpful, and some winter survival skills are recommended (i.e., basic knowledge of avalanche slope evaluation, emergency shelter construction, etc.). For the most part, elevation gain is less than 1,000 feet or, if more, the slope is gradual and relatively stable at all times. Routes may include forest trails, narrow logging roads, or moderate slope climbing.

Most difficult: These routes feature sections that will need to be evaluated for avalanche safety every time. The trails climb considerably, and there may be some slope traversing required. Hikers should have good experience and familiarity with snowshoes. These routes may include climbing to ridge tops or traverses across forested or open slopes. An ability to self-arrest with an ice ax or trekking pole is recommended.

Backcountry: These routes follow topography rather than trails or roads, so skill with a map and compass is essential. A variety of conditions may be encountered along backcountry routes, including steep elevation gains and losses. These routes require complete competence in winter survival skills, avalanche and snow condition evaluation, and some basic mountaineering skills.

Round Trip

Because snow levels vary so widely from year to year—and month to month—round-trip distances listed here are not absolute. Some of the routes begin at formal Sno-Park areas, and are therefore fairly consistent in their trip mileage, but others begin wherever the snow line is encountered, so the distances can increase or decrease by several miles based on snow accumulation. The starting points for the mileage are calculated from the average base point.

Hiking Time

Everyone moves at different speeds, but a general rule of thumb is to estimate that when walking on snowshoes, you'll be moving 30 to 50 percent slower than you would walking on a bare trail. So if you generally hike at a rate of 3 miles per hour, figure you'll be doing 1.5 to 2 miles per hour on snowshoes.

And that slower rate, combined with short winter days, means you should plan on doing fewer miles than you would if you were hiking bare trails in the summer. In fact, you should plan to cut your hiking mileage by the same 30 to 50 percent. For example, if you generally take summer dayhikes of 10 to 15 miles, plan to take snowshoe hikes of 6 to 10 miles.

Elevation Gain

Starting from the base starting point, this number is the accumulated total elevation gain from the trail's start to its high point. The total will vary if snow levels force you to start above or below the starting point listed.

High Point

This is the elevation of the highest point on the route, not necessarily the end point.

Best Hiking Time

There is only one accurate answer to the question, "When is the best time to snowshoe each route?" That answer is, "It depends." But since that's not too useful, I've put myself on the line and offered an estimate of when you'll find the best conditions for each route. Bear in mind, though, that first answer. The best time to snowshoe any given route is when the snow is stable, yet deep and fluffy; when the weather is clear and calm; and when the route is free of avalanche danger. While a trail may be great one December, it could be bare of snow the next. I've snowshoed some trails in June that I had hiked the previous June with no snow in sight. So, again, I've estimated a range for the "average" year and ask that you be open-minded with your interpretation of that range.

Maps

Not enough can be said about the importance of carrying and using good topographic maps on every outing. Winter hiking isn't like summer hiking—the trail isn't always visible. In fact, more often than not, the "trail" doesn't exist anywhere but on the map. It is your responsibility to make sure that you are on course.

The maps in this book are not designed to be used for routefinding. They are intended as locator maps to assist you in visualizing the hike and to help you locate the route on a topographic map.

To help you find the maps you need, I have also listed the Custom Correct and/or Green Trails maps covering the hiking area. This will help you make use of your existing trail maps. Custom Correct and Green Trails maps are commercially produced. While many snowshoers may have and use U.S. Geological Survey (USGS) maps—they are available

LEGEND

70	Interstate highway
24	U.S. highway
36	State highway
272	County or Forest Service road
——	Paved road or good road
═══	Gravel or dirt road
- - - -	Snowshoe trail
▲	Campground
T	Trail start
⌣	Bridge
⋏⋏	Mountain peak
～	River or creek
●	Lake or pond
→N	North
■	Building or site
⊼	Picnic area

for the entire state—I've found the commercially produced maps, when applicable, are more beneficial to recreationists. USGS maps are not updated regularly. Many of the Washington maps haven't been revised for more than 20 years, so the roads and trails listed on them may be outdated, although the geographic information is still highly accurate. On the other hand, the maps from commercial mapmakers are revised regularly, with updated trail and road information, making them more useful for recreationists.

Custom Correct offers detailed topographic maps for the Olympic Peninsula. The maps are not based on a grid system like USGS maps, but instead are designed to cover entire river valleys and/or trail networks. As such, the Custom Correct maps have a lot of overlap, but their strength is the fact that for any given hike, only one map is needed. Green Trails maps, on the other hand, are based on a grid system covering the Olympic Peninsula and the entire Cascade Range through northern Oregon.

Who to Contact

In addition to calling the Northwest Avalanche Center Hotline, it's a good idea to contact the local land manager to get current information on the specific area you plan to visit. To make it easier for you to do that, I've included the name of the agency in charge of the land traversed by each route. Addresses and phone numbers are provided in the Appendix.

A NOTE ABOUT SAFETY

Safety is an important concern in all outdoor activities. No guidebook can alert you to every hazard or anticipate the limitations of every reader. Therefore, the descriptions of roads, trails, routes, and natural features in this book are not representations that a particular place or excursion will be safe for your party. When you follow any of the routes described in this book, you assume responsibility for your own safety. Under normal conditions, such excursions require the usual attention to traffic, road and trail conditions, weather, terrain, the capabilities of your party, and other factors. Keeping informed on current conditions and exercising common sense are the keys to a safe, enjoyable outing.

—The Mountaineers

Snowshoe tracks along the river valley, Middle Fork Nooksack route

Snowshoer hiking along road to ridge, Hurricane Hill route

-- *1* --

Hurricane Hill

Rating:	Easiest to more difficult
Round trip:	6 miles
Hiking time:	4 hours
Elevation gain:	800 feet
High point:	5,760 feet
Best season:	Late December through early March
Maps:	Green Trails: Mount Olympus No. 134 and Mount Angeles No. 135; Custom Correct: Hurricane Ridge
Who to contact:	Olympic National Park

Hurricane Ridge is the preeminent destination for folks who want to see the beauty of Olympic National Park any time of the year. When winter rolls in and the broad, sweeping meadows of the ridge are blanketed in snow, and the high jagged peaks of Bailey Range are swaddled in white, the area is unbelievably beautiful. All the best—and some of the worst—aspects of snowshoeing are found here. Wide, wonderful panoramic views; alpine meadows of rolling snowdrifts; frosted evergreens and dark, brooding forests; and occasionally, frigid, scouring winds that blind all visitors with white-out conditions.

Looking south toward Mount Olympus from Hurricane Hill

Hurricane Ridge, and the snowshoe hike to Hurricane Hill, offers the best views in the park of majestic Mount Olympus. The peak so captivated early explorers with its beauty that the mountain was deemed worthy of being home to the gods.

To get there, from Port Angeles drive 17 miles up Hurricane Ridge Road to the Hurricane Ridge Visitor Center. Park near the lodge, and sign in with the rangers at the center.

Heading west from the lodge, snowshoe along the roadway as it rolls around the flank of the Hurricane Ridge meadows. The road soon enters forest and drops gently with the ridge for nearly a mile. The trail levels out along a high saddle, passing a broad picnic area near the end of the road. A brief climb from the picnic area takes you to the end of the road at 1.5 miles. At this point the real snowshoeing work begins. If you are just looking for a quiet stroll, turn back here and explore the trailside meadows on your return trip; but if you are looking for more of a challenge, continue toward Hurricane Hill.

Following the general path of the small hiker's trail west from the end of the road, snowshoe steeply up an exposed ridge line to the top of Hurricane Hill. The trail stays on the west side of the ridge, passing under two tricky avalanche chutes. Snowshoers will do better to merely stick to the narrow (sometimes, knife-edged) ridge crest all the way to the top. If the snow is heavily crusted or icy, even snowshoes with heavy cleats will not be enough to ensure safe footing, so come prepared to turn around before reaching the true summit of Hurricane Hill.

Even if the top isn't reached, the views are spectacular all along the

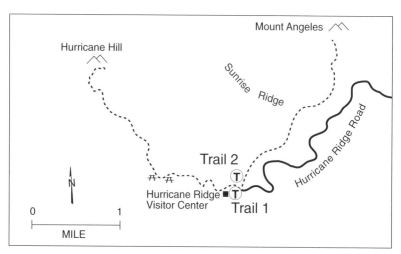

trail. To the north, the Strait of Juan de Fuca is a dark blue ribbon between the Olympic foothills and the far shore of Canada's Vancouver Island. Northeast, the San Juan Islands are seen cradled in the calm, blue waters of upper Puget Sound, with Mount Baker rearing its icy head beyond. To the east, Mount Angeles and McCarthy Peak jut up at the far side of the Olympic Mountains. To the south, Mount Olympus reigns supreme, dominating the beautiful Bailey Range.

There is beauty to behold in every direction. But there is also the possibility of danger. Weather on Hurricane Ridge is unpredictable and prone to rapid changes. Come prepared for a variety of conditions—sunny days can quickly fade into heavy fog and frigid temperatures. Calm weather can give way, in just minutes, to heavy winds and white-out conditions. Be ready for extreme conditions, and be willing to turn back the moment the weather starts to turn foul.

--2--
Mount Angeles/Heather Park

Rating:	Backcountry
Round trip:	6 miles
Hiking time:	6 hours
Elevation gain:	600 feet
High point:	5,900 feet
Best season:	Late December through early March
Maps:	Green Trails: Mount Angeles No. 135; Custom Correct: Hurricane Ridge
Who to contact:	Olympic National Park

Although little elevation gain occurs along this route, lots of work is necessary for snowshoers planning to play here. The trail starts high and stays high as it skirts steep ridges and traverses around the flanks of towering mountains. But with the hard work comes ample rewards. Stunning views of Elk Mountain, Maiden Peak, Blue Mountain, and the deep Cox Creek Valley lie off to the southeast. Above, Mount Angeles and Rocky Peak loom large. And all around the trail are picturesque scenes of winter loveliness— open meadows, frosted evergreens cradled by rolling snowdrifts, and icicles hanging like crystal fingers off rocky ledges on the mountain face.

To get there, from Port Angeles drive 17 miles up Hurricane Ridge

Snowy meadow and forest along the route to Heather Park

Road to the Hurricane Ridge Visitor Center. Park near the lodge, and sign in with the rangers at the center.

From the visitor center, snowshoe right around the downhill ski area and turn north to climb to the ridge crest above the rope-tow. Snowshoe out along the ridge crest with Mount Angeles towering dead ahead. The trail is fairly level as it pierces small stands of forest and crosses open meadows. At 1.8 miles, the route rolls under the nose of Sunrise Ridge, which stretches off to the left. The trail stays high on the narrow ridge as it passes Sunrise and crosses above a wide, open basin on the left. This pretty, forested alpine valley nestles between Sunrise Ridge and Mount Angeles. On the east side of the trail, the slope drops steeply to the Cox Creek Valley. The road to Hurricane Ridge is occasionally seen directly below the trail.

At 2.7 miles, the trail curves right across the steep flank of Mount Angeles. Continue north, leaving the trail route, and climb a quarter mile to the top of a wide bench on the southern flank of the mountain. Here, at 5,900 feet, enjoy views of the mountain while avoiding the avalanche-prone east side of Mount Angeles—the area to which the trail leads.

Plenty of opportunities are available for scrambling around the flanks of the mountain, but you will find that the slopes are steep and avalanche danger is high throughout the area when the snow isn't completely stable. Make good use of the Northwest Avalanche Center, and the avalanche information posted at the Hurricane Ridge Visitor Center, before venturing out on this trail.

-- ϟ --

Eagle Point

Rating:	Most difficult
Round trip:	10 miles
Hiking time:	7 hours to 2 days
Elevation gain:	Up to 2,500 feet
High point:	5,500 feet
Best season:	Late December through early March
Maps:	Green Trails: Mount Angeles No. 135; Custom Correct: Hurricane Ridge
Who to contact:	Olympic National Park

With the sweeping line of white mountains that ends at glacier-capped Mount Olympus stretching before them, snowshoers will wonder why they ever bothered visiting this area in the summer. The hike begins with a short, steep descent, and then wanders over fairly level terrain—just a few rolling hills—as the trail stretches east under the flank of jagged Steeple Rock and Eagle Point. Snowshoers will find great views of the distant peaks of the Bailey Range, and look down into the dark Lillian River Valley.

Snowshoers looking for a gentle outing (or if the snow is icy) can pitch their tents at Waterhole Camp—just 4 miles out. This sheltered area has plenty of views and scenery. For a more strenuous trek, push on past Waterhole, climbing along the flank of Eagle Point, before entering a long

Snowshoer climbing slope below Cathedral Peak toward Eagle Point

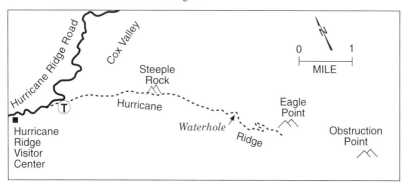

open stretch to Obstruction Point. This last 3-mile leg is treacherous in inclement weather, so pay attention to weather reports and current conditions. If a storm threatens, make camp at Waterhole and save the last leg for another time, or do it the next morning as a pre-breakfast blood-warmer if the air is clear and calm.

To get there, from Port Angeles drive 17 miles up Hurricane Ridge Road to the Hurricane Ridge Visitor Center. Sign in at the center (required for all users), and then drive back down the road a half mile to the trailhead parking area near the first bend in the road.

Start the hike from the last switchback on Hurricane Ridge Road. You will need to hike a few hundred yards back from the parking area, and then drop off the road end, descending a steep hill for about 100 yards before reaching the fairly level, wide trail leading off to the east. You'll be in high subalpine forest with frequent breaks with views south to Mount Olympus and the Lillian River Valley and northwest to Mount Angeles.

The trail skirts along a wind-swept sidehill meadow on the flank of Steeple Rock. Be careful here as the fierce winds can load up avalanche chutes and create hazardous conditions occasionally. But if the winds are calm and the weather is clear, this is also the best place to find truly grand views of the entire Bailey Range of the Olympic Mountains. Steeple Rock is passed at just under 2 miles from the parking area. In another mile, you'll pass a broad, sheltered forest clearing. This is a great place to camp, known as Waterhole Camp, or just to stop and catch your breath. Push on another half mile past Waterhole to reach the flank of Eagle Point, a 6,247-foot summit towering over the trail.

This route makes a fine outing for novice winter campers. The trail is level enough that carrying winter camping gear isn't too difficult, and the distance is short enough to be doable but not long enough to get you out into a true wilderness camp.

--4--

Mount Townsend

Rating:	Most difficult
Round trip:	10 miles
Hiking time:	7 hours to 2 days
Elevation gain:	Up to 2,500 feet
High point:	5,500 feet
Best season:	Late December through early March
Maps:	Green Trails: Tyler Peak No. 136; Custom Correct: Buckhorn Wilderness
Who to contact:	Olympic National Forest, Quilcene Ranger District

Starting with a road walk, this snowshoe trek leads through steep clearcuts, virgin forest, and up to some near-vertical alpine meadows, but throughout it all, one aspect is constant: incredible, staggering views. The vistas from the road and trail along this route include sweeping views of Mount Rainier, Upper Puget Sound, Lower Hood Canal, and all of the eastern Olympic peaks. Snowshoers can scatter out and explore untouched snow

Showshoer looking toward Mount Townsend

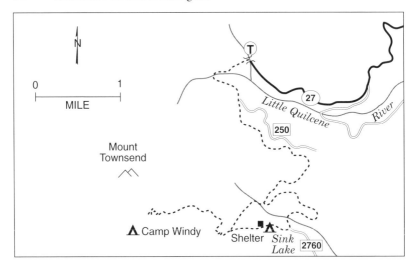

in meadows and forests well off the trail, or they can stick to the assigned path and make a nice, quiet day-hike of it. Or they can do both and spend a night or two and explore the possibilities of the slopes of Mount Townsend. The mountain itself is more of a long ridge. The summit stretches north to south and, although it's difficult to get to the top thanks to a slew of avalanche chutes, there is no shortage of scenic overlooks on which snowshoers can pause and admire the long mountain top.

To get there, from Quilcene drive north on US 101 for 1.5 miles to Lords Lake Road on the left (west). Continue up Lords Lake Road for 3 miles before turning left (south) onto Forest Service Road No. 2909 and driving 3.5 miles. At a wide road junction, turn left (the sharpest left of two possible left turns) onto Forest Service Road No. 27 and follow it through a loop curve to the west. Continue west on Road No. 27 to the point where the snow is deep enough to impede your progress, generally near the head of the Little Quilcene River Valley at 3,000 feet.

To find the best snowshoeing options, cross the Little Quilcene River via the Road No. 27 bridge and snowshoe up the road as it climbs steeply up through broad meadows (clearcuts), traverses around to the south side of the valley, and rolls south to a low saddle at 2 miles (3,700 feet). The pretty views of the first leg of the trek are supplemented here with stunning panoramas sweeping from Mount Townsend over the Quilcene River Valley, east to Puget Sound, and beyond to Mount Rainier.

The road drops from the saddle, rolls south around the nose of the ridge and, at 3.5 miles, encounters a small side road on the right. This narrow, brushy road cuts southwest for 1 mile to intercept the Mount Townsend Trail at 4.5 miles. This forested hiking path climbs steeply from the trail-head for a quarter mile before turning west on a long, climbing traverse to the base of the steep walls of the upper reaches of Mount Townsend.

Stop your climb before breaking out of the trees near the 4,500-foot level if there is even a whisper of a chance of avalanche. If the snow is extremely stable, continue to snowshoe up the trail to reach the ridge crest (5,500 feet) at 6 miles.

When the avalanche danger is moderate or higher, a better alternative for winter camping is to turn left when you encounter the Mount Townsend Trail and descend along it for a half mile to reach, at mile 5, one of the small, three-sided shelters that were so common in the Olympic Mountains in the middle half of this century.

Return the way you came or, to complete a loop, hike another half mile down the trail from the shelter to a trailhead on Road No. 27. Turn left on the road, and hike 1.5 miles up it as it curves northwest to reach the point where the spur road took off to join the upper trail.

--5--
Lena Lake/Valley of Silent Men

Rating: Backcountry
Round trip: Up to 9 miles
Hiking time: 6 hours
Elevation gain: 2,000 feet
High point: 2,800 feet
Best season: Mid-January through late February
Maps: Green Trails: The Brothers No. 168; Custom Correct: The Brothers—Mount Anderson
Who to contact: Olympic National Forest, Quilcene Ranger District

This is an unusual snowshoe outing in that, except in periods of heavy snow, the lower section of the trail may require hikers to strap their snow-shoes to their backs while they hike a mile or two up to the snow. The Lower Lena Lake Trail doesn't offer panoramic vistas, but there is a pretty forest surrounding the route, with a nice creek basin to cross and the beautiful lake to enjoy. Beyond the lake, a short excursion to the Valley of Silent Men leads snowshoers into a cathedral-like forest of massive trees, flanking a

clear, tumbling stream in a narrow valley. The ancient trees sport drooping beards of emerald green lichens and mosses, and the stream is lined with a lacy network of ice.

To get there, from Hoodsport drive 13 miles north on US 101 to a junction with Hamma Hamma Road (Forest Service Road No. 25). Turn left (west) onto Hamma Hamma Road, and continue west 8 miles to the Lena Lake Trailhead parking area on either side of the road. The trail is on the right (north) side of the road.

In heavy snow years, a thin layer of snow may be found at the trailhead (800 feet), but generally you will have to leave your 'shoes on your packs and start up the trail in your boots. The trail climbs steeply, though, and shortly after crossing Lena Creek at 1.5 miles, the snow deepens. When it is too

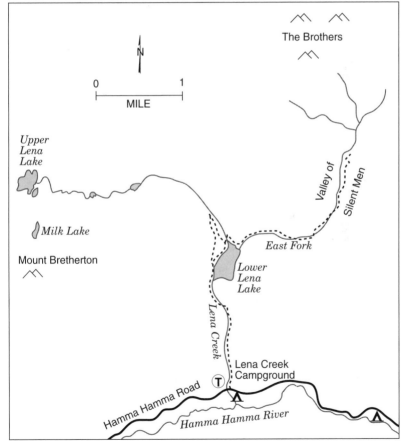

Mossy tree along the trail to Lower Lena Lake

deep, or too slick, to hike in boots, strap on the snowshoes and continue.

The trail tapers into a gentle climb at 1.6 miles and a quiet, serene forest surrounds the route. At 3 miles, the trail rolls along the west side of Lower Lena Lake (2,050 feet). Follow the lakeshore north, and turn right to cross the first inlet stream at the north end of the lake. Head east along the second inlet, East Fork Lena Creek, as it climbs into the lush ancient forest of the Valley of Silent Men. Trail signs indicate this is the climber's route to The Brothers, but generally you won't be going that far. Snowshoe up the bottom of the valley, following the trail corridor as it weaves through the trees, for up to 1.5 miles from the lake before turning back. The valley makes a great place to stop for a leisurely picnic. Sit and enjoy the quiet music of the stream tumbling over icy rocks. Listen to the songs of the birds flitting through the branches of the trees above: gray jays, as always, dominate the air when there is any chance they can beg—or steal—a meal from hikers. Relax in the soothing peace that covers all visitors to these cathedral forests, which are made all the more peaceful by the quiet wrought by winter's presence.

--6--

Coat Pass

Rating:	More difficult
Round trip:	10 miles
Hiking time:	6 hours
Elevation gain:	2,400 feet
High point:	4,750 feet
Best season:	January through early March
Maps:	Green Trails: Mount Baker No. 13
Who to contact:	Mount Baker–Snoqualmie National Forest, Mount Baker Ranger District

See page 43 for map.

For those snowshoers who like to just get out and walk for miles without worrying about the intricacies of routefinding in deep snow, the Coat Pass trek is a great option. The route follows a wide roadbed as it climbs from forested Glacier Creek Valley to the open views in Coat Pass. The road weaves through many forest clearings and crosses several creek basins before reaching its end at the 4,700-foot pass separating the twin peaks of

Lookout Mountain. From the pass, views to the southeast sweep in Mount Baker's northwest flank, from Chowder Ridge to Lincoln and Colfax Peaks, with the sprawling ice of Coleman and Roosevelt Glaciers in between.

To get there, from Bellingham drive east on State Route 542 (Mount Baker Highway) to the town of Glacier and continue another 0.7 mile, passing the U.S. Forest Service Public Service Center, before turning right (south) onto Forest Service Road No. 39 (Glacier Creek Road). Drive to the snow line, usually found near a road junction (Forest Service Road No. 3940, gated) just past Coal Creek, about 5.2 miles from Mount Baker Highway.

Strap on your snowshoes, and start the trek by following Road No. 39. Snowmobilers and skiers also use this road, so stick to the side of the trail to avoid being run down by motorists and to avoid tromping on the carefully laid tracks of skiers. The road climbs along Lookout Creek before crossing the creek and traversing south above the deep cut of Glacier Creek Gorge. In 2 miles, go right at the fork onto Forest Service Road No. 36. (The left fork leads to the Coleman Glacier Route.) The road traverses through young second-growth forest, clearcuts, and steep alder slopes before banking to the left and crossing the upper Lookout Creek Basin near the 4,500-foot level, 2 miles from the start of Road No. 36. Across Lookout Creek Basin, the road loops north, and then flips through a wide switchback to reach another road junction. Stay right (on Forest Service

Camp-robber jay (a.k.a. whiskey jack or gray jay) looking for dropped crumbs near snowshoer tracks

Road No. 3610), and climb steeply through a short series of switchbacks and a half-mile-long traverse to reach Coat Pass, just a touch over 5 miles from the Coal Creek parking area.

Soak up the views from the pass, enjoy a leisurely lunch, and then decide whether to head back or extend the outing. For more adventures, leave the Coat Pass and climb to the left (south), ascending the main peak of Lookout Mountain (5,021 feet). There is no formal trail, but climbing through the trees and meadows is easy with snowshoes. Pick the path of least resistance. The best bet is to climb steeply, but angle just a bit to the left on the ascent to avoid the steepest pitches. The summit is about a half mile from the pass. To cut the return trip mileage, drop to the east from the summit to rejoin the road about a half mile down from the pass.

--7--
Coleman Glacier

Rating:	Backcountry
Round trip:	14 miles
Hiking time:	1 to 2 days
Elevation gain:	4,500 feet
High point:	6,500 feet
Best season:	January through February
Maps:	Green Trails: Mount Baker No. 13
Who to contact:	Mount Baker–Snoqualmie National Forest, Mount Baker Ranger District

Starting with an easy stroll along a wide trail in a narrow creek valley, this trek offers a taste of all the best winter has to offer. The trail climbs away from the valley bottom after a few miles and presents two choices: a modest climb along a wide road to a high promontory with great views of Mount Baker or a longer, more strenuous climb along the narrow, forested path on Heliotrope Ridge. Both provide wonderful views, and a good stretch of the legs in deep snows, but snowshoers must share the road with skiers and snowmobilers, while the Heliotrope Ridge Trail is quiet and usually untracked. But this also means the trail is considerably more difficult to follow than the wide roadbed. Novice snowshoers will find plenty of excitement and enjoyment on the Mount Baker View trek, while more experienced backcountry snowshoers will find the trail puts their skills to good use.

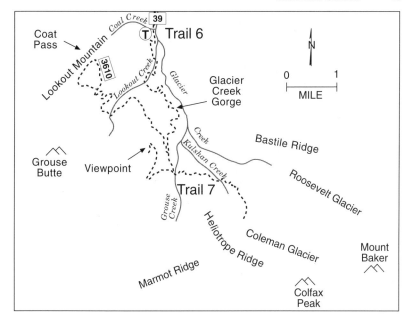

To get there, from Bellingham drive east on State Route 542 (Mount Baker Highway) to the town of Glacier and continue another 0.7 mile, passing the U.S. Forest Service Public Service Center, before turning right (south) onto Forest Service Road No. 39 (Glacier Creek Road). Drive to the snow line, usually found near a road junction (Forest Service Road No. 3940, gated) just past Coal Creek, about 5.2 miles from Mount Baker Highway.

Beginning at the snow line, follow the Glacier Creek Road up-valley. Snowmobilers and skiers also use this road, so stick to the side of the trail to avoid being run over by motorists and to avoid tromping on the carefully laid tracks of skiers. The road climbs through thick, young forest for the first half mile before crossing Lookout Creek and leveling out somewhat. A few small clearcuts offer modest views and the first opportunity to step off the track and practice some deep-snow travel techniques.

In 2 miles, the track forks. Stay to the left on Road 39, and in about a half mile, the road curves sharply to the right. The Heliotrope Ridge Trailhead is found at this corner. Turn left into the forest, and follow the trail corridor east, crossing Grouse Creek almost immediately and climbing through the shadowy woods. The trail may be difficult to find in places, so follow the widest corridor between the dark tree trunks. The route climbs steadily for a half mile before tapering into a long, ascending traverse along Heliotrope Ridge's north side. About a mile and a half after leaving the

Snowshoer and a group of cross-country skiers on the flanks of the glacier

road, cross the upper reaches of Kulshan Creek. This is the best place to establish camp if you plan to spend the night. The trees offer shelter from the wind and weather, while the views are found less than a half mile away. To get to those views, turn right on the west side of the Kulshan Creek draw and climb uphill to break out of the trees and enjoy views of Coleman Glacier and upper Heliotrope Ridge. If conditions permit, venture out on the snowfields at the edge of the glacier and explore the snowy alpine world along this wild side of Mount Baker.

For a less strenuous outing, stick to Road No. 39 at the trailhead and climb to the right along the roadway for another mile and a half. The road ends at a high viewpoint above clearcut meadows. The view of Mount Baker's northwest side, with its sprawling Coleman and Roosevelt Glaciers, is unmatched. Enjoy the view over lunch, and then if you want a change of pace, abandon the road as you start the return trip. Point the tips of your snowshoes toward Mount Baker, and drop downhill, angling slightly to the right, through the meadows and trees for a little off-trail snowshoeing before rejoining the road in a quarter mile or so.

-- 𝟪 --

White Salmon Creek

Rating: Easiest
Round trip: 10 miles
Hiking time: 6 hours
Elevation gain: 300 feet
High point: 2,400 feet
Best season: December through early March
Maps: Green Trails: Mount Shuksan No. 14
Who to contact: Mount Baker–Snoqualmie National Forest, Mount Baker Ranger District

Bring the whole family to this beautiful river valley. The wide track, with plenty of open meadows and forest glades for exploring, offers great snowshoeing for folks of all abilities. The scenery will, likewise, appeal to all. The views begin with the glorious winter landscape around the trail— picture dark, shadowy evergreens flocked with heavy white snow set beside a clear mountain river—but soon all eyes are drawn to the vista beyond. This is a narrow valley, and the mountains flanking it soar straight up into the sky. From Goat Mountain to Mount Sefrit and the Nooksack Ridge, the peaks form a ragged skyline far above the valley floor.

When venturing out this way, be sure to call the district ranger first to get a current snow report. This is a fairly low-elevation trail, and although some years 3 or 4 feet of snow may be along the trail, mild winters can find the track snow-free for much of its length. Of course, one of the conveniences of snowshoes is that regular hiking boots can be worn when walking on them. That means, when the snow is thin, just stash the snowshoes and take a winter hike.

To get there, from Bellingham drive east on State Route 542 (Mount Baker Highway) to the town of Glacier. Continue another 12.5 miles past Glacier, and turn left into the Salmon Ridge Sno-Park, which is found just past the North Fork Nooksack River Bridge.

From the Sno-Park, ramble out into the open glades along the Nooksack River, but to get in a full day of snowshoeing, head out along

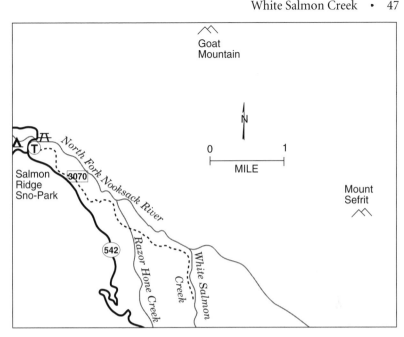

Forest Service Road No. 3070 as it parallels the picturesque river upstream. As you hike up the valley, be sure to stay off the groomed ski tracks. Volunteers groom this trail for cross-country skiers, and there is no faster way to irritate skiers than by tromping their tracks into a series of deep snowshoe depressions. But plenty of room is available here for all, and in several areas you can take off through open meadows to get well clear of the ski tracks and be off on your own. Angle off to the left in the first mile or so to get down to the river's edge for some water views. But stay back from the edge because weak snow may be overhanging the water. As you move up the valley, veer to the right to climb onto the foot of the valley wall and enter the dark cedar and hemlock forest. At 2 miles, turn sharply to the right (south) and climb a small bench for good, open views of Goat Mountain to the north. From there, traverse around the lower edge of the bench and enter the White Salmon Creek Basin. Pick a path through the trees to the edge of the creek. For an extended outing, push on upstream and continue until the trees get too tight or your legs get too tired. To keep the trek modest, turn downstream and follow the White Salmon for a quarter mile back to the main track, which ends where the White Salmon empties into the Nooksack.

Open water along White Salmon Creek

--9--
Artist Point

Rating:	More difficult
Round trip:	5.5 miles
Hiking time:	4 hours
Elevation gain:	1,200 feet
High point:	5,200 feet
Best season:	December through April
Maps:	Green Trails: Mount Shuksan No. 14
Who to contact:	Mount Baker–Snoqualmie National Forest, Mount Baker Ranger District

Artist Point may have earned its name because of the oft-captured image of the broad meadows filled with summer wildflowers, backed by the towering rock summit of Mount Shuksan and glacier-crowned Mount Baker. But many feel the area is even more beautiful and worthy of reproduction on film or canvas when shrouded with snow. The actual namesake of this trail is a high viewpoint between the two great peaks. All around the point are ancient forests, and come winter, the deep green trees are cloaked in shrouds of white as wind-driven snow and hoarfrost cling to the evergreen limbs. On overcast days, the area becomes a world of black and white, with many shades of gray. But on clear, calm days, the world is blue and white: white snow, white peaks, blue-tinted evergreens, and sapphire blue skies.

To get there, from Bellingham drive east on State Route 542 (Mount Baker Highway) to the road end, about 55 miles, at the upper parking lot of the Mount Baker Ski Area.

To start the trip, leave the south (upper) end of the ski area parking lot and edge along the flank of the downhill area along the access road to Austin Pass. Just past the ski runs, the route turns upward and you begin a long, steady climb to Austin Pass. Stay off to the right of the road to avoid cross-country skiers who are heading for the deep, backcountry bowls beyond Artist Point. The track covers 500 feet of elevation gain from the parking area to 4,700-foot Austin Pass, but that gain is easily accomplished on snowshoes—it's the side-stepping cross-country skiers who will be sweating this section.

From Austin Pass, the road sweeps out to the left in a long switchback. Keep right, and climb the open meadows ahead to cut across the neck of

Skiers and snowshoers on the meadows near Artist Point

this loop, rejoining the road and trail in a few hundred yards at the road end at the lower end of Kulshan Ridge, just past the 2-mile mark. A final quarter mile of hiking to the left along this ridge gets you to the impossibly beautiful views at Artist Point. Soak in the views of Mount Shuksan to the east, Mount Baker to the west, and to the southwest, Coleman Pinnacle towers seemingly just beyond reach. Backcountry telemark skiers are often seen playing in the steep, deep snowbowls along Ptarmigan Ridge, which stretches between Artist Point and Coleman Pinnacle. This ridge is filled with dangerous avalanche chutes, so before deciding to trek out along it, be sure of the current avalanche conditions. A better option for an extended trek from Artist Point is to the left (east) along the more stable snow of Kulshan Ridge. A half mile of hiking along the deep snow on the ridge crest leads to Huntoon Point, a high knob on the upper end of Kulshan. From this lofty observation point, look out over the expanse of the Mount

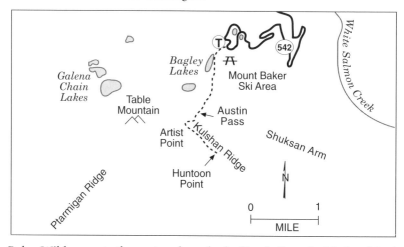

Baker Wilderness to the west and south, the North Cascades National Park (which encompasses Mount Shuksan) to the east, and the ragged line of Shuksan Arm—reaching out from Shuksan—to the north.

--*10*--

Middle Fork Nooksack

Rating:	Backcountry
Round trip:	7 miles
Hiking time:	5 hours
Elevation gain:	900 feet
High point:	3,000 feet
Best season:	December through early February
Maps:	Green Trails: Hamilton No. 45
Who to contact:	Mount Baker–Snoqualmie National Forest, Mount Baker Ranger District

The most difficult part of this snowshoe hike is getting to the snow. But once the network of roads has been safely navigated, the fun can begin in earnest. This is a largely untouched winter wilderness setting, and finding solitude amid such staggering beauty is remarkable. The trail follows the Middle Fork Nooksack upstream in the very shadow of majestic Mount

Snow-covered trees along the Middle Fork Nooksack route

Baker. When tired of viewing that big volcano, glance right and soak in the beauty of Loomis Mountain.

On the return trip, Mount Baker is at the back, but the twin towers of Sisters Mountain loom ahead. In the midst of all this mountain scenery lives an array of wild creatures for snowshoers to quietly observe. Snowshoe hares, ptarmigans—large grouselike birds that turn snowy white come winter—martens, weasels, foxes, and blacktail deer thrive in this valley. Of course, with all those prey-animals living here, predators are close at hand. Bobcats, lynx (one of the last population of lynx in Washington), cougars, coyotes, and possibly even wolves roam these woods. These critters pose little danger to healthy, adult humans, and any encounter with them should be counted as a blessing.

To get there, from Bellingham drive east on State Route 542 (Mount Baker Highway) for 18 miles before turning right onto Mosquito Lake Road (about 2 miles north of the junction of Mount Baker Highway and State Route 9 at Deming). Drive 5 miles east on Mosquito Lake Road, and then turn left (east) onto Forest Service Road No. 38. Continue 11 miles east on Road No. 38 to a junction with a small spur road (2,000-feet elevation) on the right signed as the access to Elbow Lake Trail. Depending on snow levels, park here, or in light snow years, continue up the main road another 2 miles to a switchback. The trailhead is found at the apex of this switchback corner.

Most years, the snow is at or below the Elbow Lake Trailhead parking area, so start from there and hike the 2 miles up Road No. 38 to the Middle Fork Trailhead. Relax and enjoy the scenery along this road, which is nearly level and well graded. Mount Baker dominates the northeast horizon, and the wide bed of the Middle Nooksack River is a constant source of entertainment to your right. The river weaves in and out of gravel bars and small forested islands. The snow-lined banks provide a crisp edge to the tumbling waters of the river.

At the first hairpin turn in the road, go straight to find the trail at the point of the switchback. The trail continues to follow the river upstream, while the road climbs the hill away from the river. The trail is narrow, and if the snow isn't deep, there may be a few downed trees to scramble over. This trail is seldom maintained, and fallen trees are nearly always present. However, the trees are more a hindrance to skiers than snowshoers, and they help to ensure solitude on this beautiful trail.

The next 1.5 miles of trail parallel the river, and the views remain largely unchanged: where the forest is open, Mount Baker, Loomis Mountain, and Park Butte dominate the skyline; where the forest canopy closes in, the beautiful old-growth forest and sparkling river will captivate you.

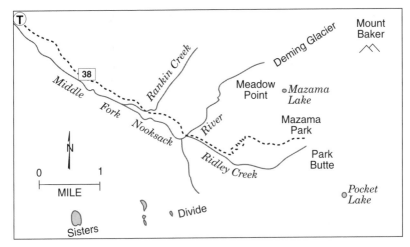

At 3.5 miles (3,200 feet), the trail begins to climb toward Mazama Park on the southwest flank of Mount Baker. The trail, though, is difficult to follow as it traverses several avalanche slopes and dips into areas of dense forest. Better to just enjoy the views, and turn back when the trail turns vertical.

--11--

Schriebers Meadow

Rating:	More difficult
Round trip:	10 to 15 miles
Hiking time:	1 to 2 days
Elevation gain:	1,200 feet
High point:	5,200 feet
Best season:	January through March
Maps:	Green Trails: Hamilton No. 45 and Lake Shannon No. 46
Who to contact:	Mount Baker–Snoqualmie National Forest, Mount Baker Ranger District

Depending on the starting snow elevation, this may be a wonderful day hike in wide meadows or a long, overnight trek through forests before reaching those alpine clearings. Regardless, this route is a jewel for winter enthusiasts. Expect to share the road and trail with cross-country skiers and probably a few snowmobilers, although midweek or after mid-January (after the typical holiday rush to the hills) finds the setting tranquil and uncrowded. But even if others are along the route, there is plenty of wild country and beautiful scenery for all to share. The great white cone of Mount Baker looms over the trail to the north, while the undulating snowfields of Schriebers Meadow are broad enough to beckon one and all out into the untracked expanses for a moment of wintry solitude.

To get there, from Sedro Woolley drive east on US 20 for 14 miles before turning left (north) onto Forest Service Road No. 11 (Baker Lake Road). Drive north on Road No. 11 for 12.5 miles, and then turn left onto Forest Service Road No. 12. Continue on Road No. 12 for 3.5 miles to the Sno-Park at the junction of Road No. 12 and Forest Service Road No. 13. If snow conditions permit, turn right and drive up Road No. 13 to the snow line (typically about 3 more miles, near the 2,500- to 3,000-foot elevation).

If the snow is heavy, park at the Sno-Park at the junction of Roads No. 12 and No. 13 and begin a 5-mile trek along the wide, forested corridor of Road No. 13. This leads up a pair of switchbacks before tapering in a long, climbing traverse along the hillside above Sulphur Creek. The road ends at a broad parking area marking the trailhead of the Schriebers Meadow–Park Butte Trail. This 5-mile road section provides a good stretch of the legs without an excessive workout, leaving you with plenty of energy for snowshoeing through the wondrous meadows above.

At the road end, the route jumps onto the narrow trail, crossing Sulphur Creek before climbing in a short quarter mile to the lower edge of Schriebers Meadow. This broad, undulating world of white is a paradise

Foggy forest at the edge of Schriebers Meadow

of winter recreation. Skiers are sure to be found slashing down the slopes flanking the meadows, and on busy Saturdays in January, expect to hear the whine of a few snowmobiles, too. To find solitude, angle off into the untracked reaches of the meadows. To the south, climb up a moderate slope for a quarter mile or so to reach a basin with three or four ice-covered alpine tarns. Here the views of Mount Baker are at their ultimate best, and good campsites are found in this area, too. Just pick a spot big enough for a tent on the leeward side of the hill, with a glade of trees flanking it for added shelter from storms in February.

Another alternative is to push on for a longer snowshoe trek by crossing the flat meadows to the northwest and then starting a gradual climb between two long rocky ridges. These ridges are lateral moraines—rock piles that were pushed aside by flowing glaciers. Climb this wide trough, and in about 1.5 miles from the end of the road, cross the upper reaches of Rocky Creek. Use care here because the many seemingly solid snow-bridges

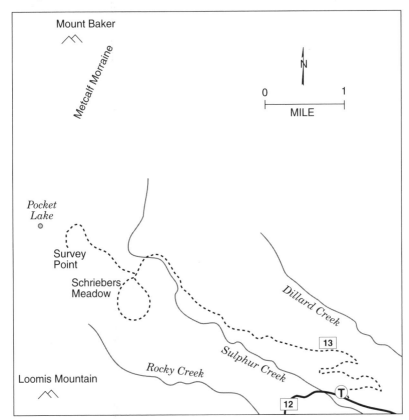

may be weak and unsafe, especially late in the season or after periods of unusually warm weather. After you cross the creek, the climbing is steep and steady for another half mile. Then bear left (west), and traverse a long, open slope to reach the top of the ridge of the left-hand moraine for stunning views of Mount Baker, the sprawling white blanket of Schriebers Meadow, and the high peaks of Park and Black Buttes to the west.

--12--
Sauk Mountain

Rating:	Backcountry
Round trip:	11 miles
Hiking time:	8 hours
Elevation gain:	3,500 feet
High point:	5,500 feet
Best season:	Late December through early February
Maps:	Green Trails: Darrington No. 78 and Lake Shannon No. 46
Who to contact:	Mount Baker–Snoqualmie National Forest, Darrington Ranger District

Although this snowshoe trek makes use of a road for much of the route's length, the way is steep, generally icy, and the upper section follows narrow, avalanche-prone hiking trails. But when conditions are good, the physical exertion needed to tromp up this steep-sloped peak is richly rewarded with stunning views of the jagged crests of a multitude of North Cascade peaks. Glacier Peak dominates the horizon, but the landscape closer at hand is just as lovely. Because of the frequent, frigid winds, the vegetation of exposed meadows on the upper slopes of Sauk is usually glazed with frilly ice-lacing. Hoarfrost, formed by wind-driven moisture and cold air temperatures, creates delicate icy ornamentation on limbs, leaves, and—when they stand still too long—snowshoers.

To get there, from Sedro Woolley drive east on US 20 (North Cascades Highway) to the town of Concrete. Continue east another 6.5 miles, and turn left (north) onto Sauk Mountain Road (Forest Service Road No. 1030). If you pass Rockport State Park, you've gone too far. (Turn around, and

Small drift on the upper flank of Sauk Mountain

drive 200 yards west of the park to find the Sauk Mountain Road junction.) Drive north on Sauk Mountain Road to the snow line—generally about 1.5 miles up the road, near a junction at the 1,400-foot level.

After turning around and parking well off the main road, continue up the roadway on snowshoes. The road repeatedly switchbacks as it climbs relentlessly for another mile through open clearcut meadows and thin patches of second-growth forest. The road continues to climb, now in heavy second-growth timber, until, near the 4-mile mark, views reveal stunning peaks down into the perpetually mist-laden Sauk River Valley and southwest toward Glacier Peak. Keep hiking along the wind-swept road as it rolls along the flank of Sauk Mountain to a final switchback corner at about 4.5 miles. Here Puget Sound is brought into view. From this point, near 3,600-feet elevation, the road climbs back toward the west to a point directly below the summit of the mountain. This stretch crosses several avalanche chutes and should be attempted only when avalanche dangers can be confirmed as minimal.

On days when the snow is stable, push on the last mile to the end of the road and the start of the summer hiking trail to the summit of Sauk. The summit should be approached only by advanced winter mountaineers because the upper slopes are icy, steep, and prone to rock- and snowslides.

When avalanche dangers are moderate or higher, turn around at the last switchback, or to add a couple of miles to the outing, bear northwest on a small spur road that leads out onto Jackman Ridge. This partially logged ridge is largely unremarkable, but the trail along its crest is mostly level for its 1-mile length, and some excellent views of the upper Puget Sound Basin are found along the way.

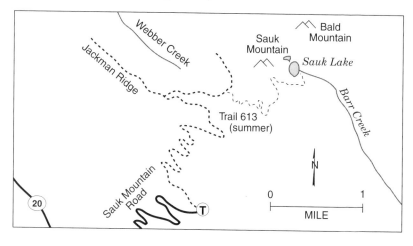

--*13*--

Iron Mountain

Rating:	Backcountry
Round trip:	9 miles
Hiking time:	8 hours
Elevation gain:	1,800 feet
High point:	4,000 feet
Best season:	January through early March
Maps:	Green Trails: Oso No. 77
Who to contact:	Mount Baker–Snoqualmie National Forest, Darrington Ranger District

This area won't be looked at twice by wilderness seekers in summer months, but when blanketed in snow, the narrow logging roads and gentle slopes are magically transformed into a pristine wilderness. There are no awesome views of scores of high peaks over beautiful wilderness rivers, but the scenery is lovely and very enjoyable. Just trekking through a quiet forest blanketed in a heavy quilt of snow is reward enough for this snowshoer.

Snowshoers with excellent routefinding skills can cut cross-country

Forest clearing on the cross-country route to Iron Mountain

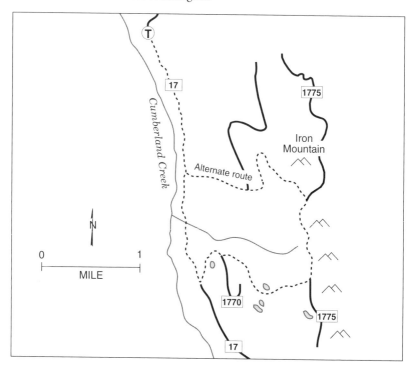

through forest and meadow to climb high onto the flanks of Iron Mountain. Meanwhile, less experienced winter travelers can stick to the roadway
for several miles. Bear in mind that snowmobilers frequent the roads in
the area on weekends, so weekdays may be the best time to visit. Also, although snowshoers hiking cross-country will find the climb to Iron Mountain quiet and snowmobile-free, snow machines may be near the summit
because a long, looping road leads nearly to the top of the mountain.

To get there, from Sedro Woolley drive south on State Route 9 across
the Skagit River Bridge and immediately turn left (east) onto South Skagit
Highway. Drive east along the South Skagit Highway as it parallels the river
upstream. In about 12 miles, turn right (south) onto Forest Service Road No.
17 and follow it south as it climbs the Cumberland Creek Valley. Drive to
the snow line, usually at least 5 miles up the road, near the 2,000-foot level.

Start up the road as it climbs gradually but steadily for the next 2.5
miles. The route slices across a few small clearcuts and pierces some dense,
second-growth forest before reaching a junction with Forest Service Road
No. 1770 on the left. Snowshoe up this short spur road as it curves north
and then turns back to the east. After a mile on this road, 3.5 miles from

the start, the trail curves back to the north. Leave the road here, and climb through the young forest, angling up the slope. There is no trail here, so simply pick the path of least resistance while always going up and slightly to the left (north). The forest here is mixed, with some young second-growth among thinner, old forests and open meadows.

About a mile of snowshoeing from the end of the road, after gaining about 450 feet in elevation, cross the wide path of Forest Service Road No. 1775 at the top of the ridge. This road meanders for several miles along the ridge crest. Turn left and follow it north as it approaches the high peak of Iron Mountain. About a mile up the ridge, 5.5 miles from the start of the hike, the road forks. The left fork slants out along the southwest side of the mountain; the right fork, the main road, curves around the eastern flank of the peak. There is no easy approach to the summit proper, but this junction is a good turnaround point. Enjoy the views from the ridge, including some nice views west toward Puget Sound, before heading back.

Time and distance can be saved with some effort by dropping off the road and heading west through the forest immediately. This means dropping down the slope at a steeper angle than where it was climbed, but the main trail, Road No. 17, is directly downhill from Road No. 1775. No matter where you drop off, just head straight downhill, being careful to avoid rocky promontories and tight thickets of brush, to catch Road No. 17.

--14--
Segelsen Ridge

Rating:	Easiest to more difficult
Round trip:	5 to 15 miles
Hiking time:	6 hours to 2 days
Elevation gain:	2,500 feet
High point:	4,516 feet
Best season:	January through February
Maps:	Green Trails: Darrington No. 78
Who to contact:	Mount Baker–Snoqualmie National Forest, Darrington Ranger District

This route is one of the lower elevation trails, so the best time to strap on snowshoes for a walk on Segelsen Ridge is in midwinter when the snow is at its deepest. Although better snow is oftentimes found elsewhere, this

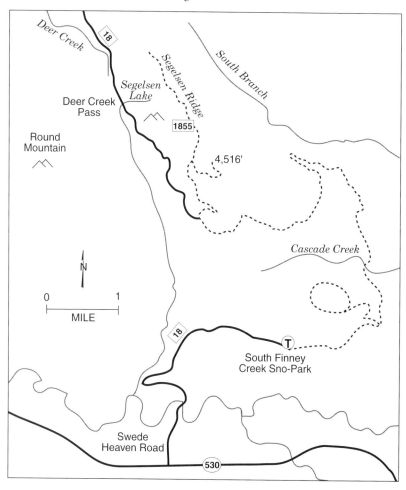

popular ridge hike offers great views without a long drive on mountain roads. The ridge is long and winding, so even on the busiest of winter weekends, there is plenty of country for all comers. In the course of a day (or for those looking to cover all of the ridge country, a long weekend), the recreationists quickly disperse along the trail. On the long downhill sections, skiers flit past trudging snowshoers; on the equally long ascents, skiers waddle up the roads spraddle-legged, stomping herringbone patterns in the snow, while snowshoers gracefully hike past them.

To get there, from Arlington drive east on State Route 530 (Mountain Loop Highway) for 24.5 miles. Near the Whitehorse Mercantile, turn left (north) onto Swede Heaven Road. Continue 2 miles north, and then bear right onto Forest Service Road No. 18 and drive to the snow line. Most years that is at least 3 miles up Road No. 18 at the South Finney Creek Sno-Park (elevation 1,200 feet), but usually it is more like 6.5 miles, just past the 2,000-foot elevation point at Cascade Creek. Hiking mileage listed here begins at the Sno-Park.

Whether on a day hike or a long overnight trip, start snowshoeing up Road No. 18, and at 2 miles above the Sno-Park, the first choice presents itself. Straight ahead lies the main road and the long ridge route it leads to. To the left is a narrow old road winding steeply up through young second-growth and some small clearcuts to the crest of a 2,685-foot un-named knob. When the snow is deep, this road offers a chance to get away from the crowds, as well as providing a good workout, nice views, and a full day of snowshoeing. The climb to the knob's summit and back to your car covers about 8 miles. Those choosing this lesser-used trail will find that the narrow jeep road divides a mile after leaving Road No. 18. Stay left, and traverse around the knob, staying just below the summit. The road soon loops back to the right (north) and climbs the western flank of the hill. To reach the true summit, leave the roadway about 1.5 miles from Road No. 18 and climb the moderately steep forested slope to the crown of the hill. Push on to the south-ern edge of the summit crown for some nice views over the Stillaguamish River Valley to Whitehorse Mountain beyond.

Snowshoers on the road section of the route

For a more extended outing, ignore this side trip and instead press on up Road No. 18 as it banks to the left, crosses the Cascade Creek Valley, and continues to climb north toward the snout of Segelsen Ridge. The views along this stretch of the trek are limited, but the occasional clearcut slope allows some peeks up the valley to the long ridge and down the valley to Whitehorse Mountain.

At 5 miles, the road takes a hard switchback to the left and rolls around the snout of Segelsen Ridge before entering the final climbing traverse toward the ridge crest. The fastest way to the top of the ridge is via a small access road, Forest Service Road No. 1855, found some 6.5 miles from the Sno-Park. Turn right, and climb the narrow, winding Road No. 1855 toward the crest. This trail switches back once about a mile above Road No. 18, and then slants steeply upward for another mile or so. Here, 2 miles above Road No. 18, leave the trail and climb a tiny two-track trail for a quarter mile along a climbing traverse before abandoning all tracks and climbing cross-country, up through trees, about 400 yards to the southern summit of the ridge crest (elevation 4,516 feet).

To extend the trip even more, return to the spur Road No. 1855 and continue upslope to the uneven crest of Segelsen Ridge. Head north along this ridge line for another 2 miles, all the while enjoying the stunning views of the surrounding countryside of open meadows, as well as the distant vistas sweeping over Whitehorse Mountain, Round Mountain, and Stillaguamish Valley.

--*15*--

Rat Trap Pass

Rating:	More difficult
Round trip:	7.5 miles
Hiking time:	6 hours
Elevation gain:	1,900 feet
High point:	3,500 feet
Best season:	December through February
Maps:	Green Trails: Sloan Peak No. 111
Who to contact:	Mount Baker–Snoqualmie National Forest, Darrington Ranger District

This little pass bridges the gap between Crystal Creek Valley to the south and Straight Creek Valley to the north. Come summer, the area is a bleak

Heading down from Rat Trap Pass

little saddle scarred by clearcuts and a narrow dusty road. But dump several feet of snow on the pass to mask the ugly logging scars, and Rat Trap Pass becomes a stunning little alpine world. High, rocky cliffs cradle snow-filled meadows and picturesque little groves of juvenile fir and hemlock. The climb to the pass is pretty enough to make the journey enjoyable, if not overly remarkable, but it's the destination that makes this snowshoe hike one to remember. By mid-December, Rat Trap Pass offers snowshoers a wide world of snowy exploration. Climb through open fields of snow to find secluded little playgrounds blocked off from other pass visitors by the rolling landscape and remnant stands of forest. Enjoy a midday repast with stunning views of the wintry landscape all around. White Chuck Mountain towers over the pass to the west, while the eastern skyline is punctuated by the craggy tops of Circle Peak and Meadow Mountain.

To get there, from Darrington drive southeast on the Mountain Loop Highway (State Route 530) for 9 miles before turning left (east) onto Forest Service Road No. 23 (White Chuck River Road). Continue east on Road No. 23 for 5 miles before crossing the White Chuck River. Drive another mile after the river crossing to the junction with Forest Service Road 27. Turn left onto Road 27, and park in the broad area near the road junction, or drive north along Road No. 27 to the snow line.

From the road junction, hike up the road, staying clear of the ever-present ski tracks, as it climbs north up a secondary valley above the White Chuck River. In less than a mile, the route crosses Crystal Creek and climbs in a half mile to the first clearing. Here, look southwest for an open view of

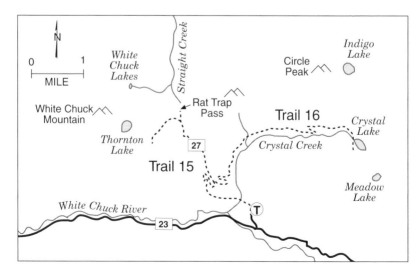

the snow-crowned monolith of Glacier Peak. Stick to the roadway for another 2 miles, passing Crystal Creek Road (Road No. 2710) at 2.5 miles from the parking area, to gain the lower reaches of the meadows surrounding Rat Trap Pass. Along this stretch, the route climbs a long traverse with periodic open views of White Chuck Mountain in front of you on the left.

Once at the meadows of the pass, angle off to the left for the best views and thinnest crowds. A small road cuts up the moderate slope, but pick a destination on the opposite side of the snowy fields and angle toward it. Climb the slopes, slicing through the few stands of mature forest and around the jumble of juvenile trees scattered here and there until reaching a suitable spot for lunch. Your picnic spot may be just beyond the main trail leading into the pass, halfway up the hillside on the western wall of the pass, or at the farthest, along the narrow draw that holds the frozen waters of Straight Creek at the far northern edge of the Rat Trap Pass meadows.

--16--
Crystal Lake

Rating:	Backcountry
Round trip:	11 miles
Hiking time:	1 to 2 days
Elevation gain:	2,800 feet
High point:	4,485 feet
Best season:	January through February
Maps:	Green Trails: Sloan Peak No. 111
Who to contact:	Mount Baker–Snoqualmie National Forest, Darrington Ranger District

With its many open views back toward Pugh Mountain, this trail offers an exceptional weekend outing in the winter wilderness. The trail begins gently enough, climbing along a wide, moderately pitched road. It then turns up a secondary valley and crawls along a narrower, steeper road. Finally, the route becomes a narrow, winding single-track trail in a dark, old forest. This section is not for the fainthearted nor for untested navigators. The trail is often hard to find, and snowshoers have to trust their skills with map, compass, and common-sense navigation to wend their way up the valley to the pretty little alpine lake lying between Circle Peak and Meadow Mountain.

Those who expend the considerable effort to hike the trail are amply

Lakeshore meadow

rewarded. Along the way, the views and local scenery are magnificent: from sweeping panoramas that take in Pugh and White Chuck Mountains to up-close and personal encounters with the deep gray-green forest of old fir, hemlock, and cedar wrapped in a cloak of snow and frost. Snowshoers will leave most of the ski traffic behind as they peel away from the main track to Rat Trap Pass and angle up the side valley of Crystal Creek and its headwaters at Crystal Lake. With fewer folks crowding the trail, the wildlife is more visible—the ever-present whiskey jack whistles all along the trail, while weasels, ptarmigans, and even a few sly foxes have been spotted along the route as well.

To get there, from Darrington drive southeast on the Mountain Loop Highway (State Route 530) for 9 miles before turning left (east) onto Forest Service Road No. 23 (White Chuck River Road). Continue east on Road No. 23 for 5 miles before crossing the White Chuck River. Drive another mile after the river crossing to the junction with Forest Service Road 27. Turn left onto Road 27, and park in the broad area near the road junction, or drive north along Road No. 27 to the snow line.

From the road junction, hike up the road as if heading toward Rat Trap Pass. The first 2.5 miles offer some nice views of Glacier Peak, Pugh Mountain, and the White Chuck River Valley from a gentle trail. At the junction of Road No. 27 and the smaller Forest Service Road No. 2710, go right onto the side road to begin the climb up into Crystal Creek Valley. The road switches back a time or two, climbing some 500 feet in less than half a mile before rolling into a long traverse up the valley. The road stays well above the creek itself, but the steep side-walls above the road provide their own problems. Snow conditions must be scrupulously checked before entering this valley because a high degree of avalanche danger exists when snow conditions are right.

The road forks in 1.5 miles from the Road No. 27 junction. Stay left to remain on the north side of Crystal Creek—the right fork slants down across the valley and then rolls out into a long, looping traverse above the White Chuck River. The trail to Crystal Lake becomes narrower at the fork, but it holds fairly level as it continues to traverse up-valley to the road end, nearly 1.5 miles past the last fork. The summer trailhead of the Crystal Lake Trail is found at the road end. The trail is a faint, seldom-maintained path that is difficult enough to find in August. Come winter, the path is visible only as an often-indistinct corridor through the trees. If the trail is lost below the snow, just pick the path of least resistance through the trees, staying on the north side of the creek, while climbing gradually to the 4,400-foot level. In about a mile, at 4,400-feet elevation, the creek turns right as it drops over a modest falls. At this point the trail is down close to the creek banks, but it remains on the north side of the water until right before the lake is reached—about a quarter mile above the falls. Crystal Lake is at 4,485 feet, and from its shores, Circle Peak, Meadow Mountain, and the crown of White Chuck Mountain are visible. The lake basin offers plenty of fine sites for camping. Crystal Lake is seldom frozen solid enough for safe travel across it, so stick to the shorelines to prevent an unwanted plunge into the icy waters.

--17--
Kennedy Hot Springs

Rating: Backcountry
Round trip: 11 miles
Hiking time: 1 to 2 days
Elevation gain: 1,050 feet
High point: 3,330 feet
Best season: Late January through late February
Maps: Green Trails: Glacier Peak No. 112 and Sloan Peak No. 111
Who to contact: Mount Baker–Snoqualmie National Forest, Darrington Ranger District

It's difficult to truly appreciate a natural hot spring unless snow is on the ground. That holds doubly true for Kennedy Hot Springs. The warm pools are a nice reward for the long, cold snowshoe trek along the White Chuck River. But without the snow to make the trail tough come winter, the

Snow- and ice-laden stream along the trail to Kennedy Hot Springs

reward would not be as pleasant. These warm springs would be just as crowded—and therefore uninviting—as they are in the summer.

Kennedy Hot Springs gets so much public pressure in the warm months that by early August, the slow-flowing springs can't flush the litter and bacteria out fast enough. After a few months of little or no use in late autumn, the pools are clear and relatively clean again—ready once more to ease the aching muscles of the snowshoers who struggle into the steaming basin. Still, it's advised that bathers avoid dunking their heads underwater as there may be lingering bacteria that, although unable to penetrate our tough skins, could find a home in the sensitive mucus membranes of the nose and eyes. Also, be aware that traditionally, Kennedy Hot Springs is clothing optional, so be prepared for bare encounters. Likewise, if kids are present in the springs, bathers should refrain from baring all until the tykes are taken back to camp by their parents. Common sense and courtesy are key to hot springs harmony.

To get there, from Darrington drive southeast on the Mountain Loop Highway (State Route 530) for 9 miles before turning left (east) onto Forest Service Road No. 23 (White Chuck River Road). Continue east on Road No. 23 for 11 miles to the road end and the trailhead parking area for the White Chuck River Trail. In periods of heavy snow, it may be necessary to park farther down the valley and snowshoe up the road a few miles. Most years, however, the road is driveable to the road end or within a mile of it. (Elevation at road end is 2,300 feet.)

The White Chuck River Trail is narrow and follows the base of the steep north wall of the valley. There are several areas where avalanches can and do occur, so extreme caution must be used in evaluating the snow and avalanche potential. (Be sure to call the Avalanche Hotline before leaving on this hike.) The trail begins with a brushy trudge through alder along the banks of the White Chuck River before slanting up-slope. At about a half mile from the trailhead, the route climbs the valley wall above the river and begins a 5-mile traverse of the hillside to the hot springs. Along the way, there are several creeks to cross and at least two tricky slide-areas to negotiate.

The first creek crossing comes nearly a mile and a half from the trailhead. Fire Creek is crossed at 2,500-feet elevation and poses little difficulty. Shortly past the creek, near the 2-mile mark, Pumice Creek is crossed, and the first avalanche/mudslide area is encountered. There is usually a jumble of brush, boulders, some downed trees, and an open scar of snow-free mud on the hillside which has sloughed off onto the trail. If the tangle of debris is especially thick, it is sometimes necessary to slip out of your snowshoes to avoid entangling the straps in the branches and sticks protruding from the slide material. Other times, there is enough snow to cover the mess. In these cases, hurry over the snow-laden piles because although the snow means easier travel, it also has the potential for an avalanche.

Just a half mile past this first debris field is another steep slope and slide area. This time, though, instead of the slope terminating in a jumble of debris, it runs out into the river. This is the trickiest part of the trail. If the snow is thin and well packed, it's possible to follow the narrow trail across this steep slope—careful use of an ice axe and a safety line is recommended at all times. But if the snow is deep or even a little unstable, it's better not to risk a slide down into the icy waters of the river. Instead, backtrack a few dozen yards until you can angle uphill through the trees to reach the top of a slanting bench that crosses over the slide area. Turn parallel to the trail, and traverse the slope above the slide area; then carefully angle back down through the thick trees to the trail.

Once you are back on the trail, it's fairly smooth snowshoeing the last 3 miles to the hot springs. At just past the 4-mile mark, the trail does a quick one-two through a pair of switchbacks, getting you up to the 3,100-foot level for a 1.5-mile-long traverse into the Kennedy Creek Basin. Cross a small side branch of the White Chuck River, another unnamed rivulet emptying into the river, and finally Kennedy Creek to reach a small ranger cabin near the springs and plenty of flat campsites nearby. To get to the springs from the campsites, cross a narrow, snow-laden bridge over the White Chuck River and turn up-river to find the soaking pools about 20 yards beyond the bridge. Be careful around the pools, as bathers hopping out of the soothing waters drip all over the snow and rocks and the pools' edges. This water then freezes, creating a treacherous coating of ice around the springs (and frequently along the trail back to the campsites). It's a good idea to use trekking poles or ice axes when walking to and from the springs.

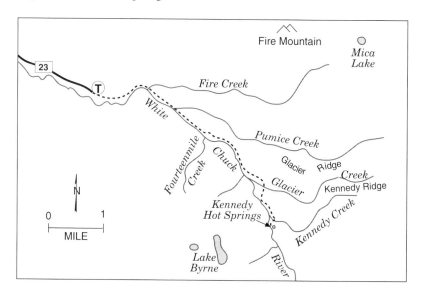

--18--
Mount Pilchuck

Rating: Easiest to more difficult
Round trip: 13 miles
Hiking time: 10 hours
Elevation gain: 2,600 feet
High point: 4,000 feet
Best season: Late January through late February
Maps: Green Trails: Granite Falls No. 109
Who to contact: Mount Pilchuck State Park
See page 76 for map.

Mount Pilchuck is a popular haven for summer hikers, but many snow-shoers fail to appreciate the challenges offered by the steep, snow-laden slopes of the mountain. That's their mistake. Mount Pilchuck offers several miles of gently climbing trail that follows the winding road leading to the summer trailhead parking area. Farther up the trail, adventurous snowshoers can forsake the roadway and hike up through the trees or along the wide runs of an abandoned downhill ski area. The alpine skiers swarmed here in the 1970s, but the resort failed after just a few years, leaving broad slopes for snowshoers to climb and telemark skiers to swoosh down. From the top of the runs, the Stillaguamish River Valley—including the deep, dark cut of Robe Gorge—sprawls below while the jagged top of Pilchuck looms overhead.

To get there, from Granite Falls drive east on the Mountain Loop Highway 1 mile past the Verlot Public Service Center and turn right (south) onto Mount Pilchuck Road (Forest Service Road No. 42). Continue up the road 1.6 miles to reach the winter closure gate. Park in the wide areas near the gate, but do not block the main road or any side access (private) roads.

The vehicle gate marks the end of all legal motorized traffic, so after snowshoeing around it, enter a world of default wilderness. The road climbs steadily but not too steeply along its first 2 miles. Off-road rambling isn't recommended in this early stage, but about 3.5 miles up the trail—just after crossing a small stream—there is an opportunity in heavy snow years to angle up through the trees to the left, cutting across the neck of a wide switchback. This will require some routefinding skills because there is no true trail. However, the trees are widely spaced enough that, if the undergrowth is buried in enough snow, you can simply climb between them.

If you prefer to keep things simple and serene, continue around on the

Hoarfrost-coated tree

road. At just over 4 miles, the road switches back to the left. A half mile farther up the route, the road turns back to the right, but if the snow is stable and avalanche dangers are minimal, a better option awaits. From the corner of the switchback, head straight out toward the west in a climbing traverse of the snowy slope on the flank of Pilchuck. In less than half a mile, the first open run of the old ski area is encountered. Climb up this wide trail, sticking to the edge near the trees to avoid a nasty confrontation (i.e., collision) with backcountry skiers practicing their telemark turns on the open slopes.

By using this steep, direct approach, the climb to the top is more of a workout, but it cuts nearly a mile off the road distance. It will also get you to the top before the crowds of skiers can kick their way up the road. That means more time at the top—the end of the road and the site of the old ski lodge—to enjoy the views alone and uninterrupted. The lodge is long gone, but the views of the Stillaguamish River Valley and the high, serrated ridges above it are as beautiful as ever.

If you have a mountaineering background and advanced avalanche-recognition skills, you might consider climbing part way up the Mount Pilchuck Trail. The route is steep and difficult to find as it winds its way up through forests, rocky slopes, and dangerous avalanche chutes. This added adventure isn't for the fainthearted or the untested—summer hikers often get lost here. So if you are an inexperienced snowshoer, stay on the slopes below the old ski area.

--19--
Heather Lake

Rating:	More difficult
Round trip:	4 miles
Hiking time:	4 hours
Elevation gain:	1,100 feet
High point:	2,440 feet
Best season:	Early January to late February
Maps:	Green Trails: Granite Falls No. 109
Who to contact:	Mount Pilchuck State Park
	See page 76 for map.

The Heather Lake Trail can be a wonderful route for snowshoers as it climbs just 2 miles—gaining over 1,000 feet—through thick second-growth forest

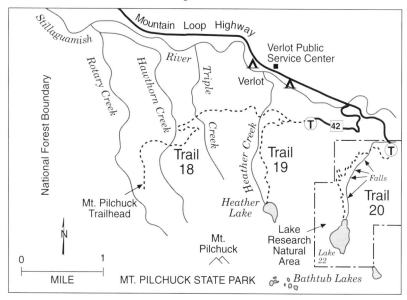

to arrive at a stunningly beautiful alpine lake nestled in a deep, rock cirque on the north face of Mount Pilchuck. The trail is heavily traveled in the summer, but winter visitors will find the crowds thin and the forests even more beautiful when blanketed in soft white. The lake features several excellent campsites around its perimeter, each with its own charm and glorious view of Mount Pilchuck or the Stillaguamish Valley. The short distance means this is a great destination to consider for first-timers in the art of winter camping.

To get there, from Granite Falls drive east on the Mountain Loop Highway (State Route 530) 1 mile past the Verlot Public Service Center and turn right (south) onto Mount Pilchuck Road (Forest Service Road No. 42). Continue up the road 1.6 miles to reach the winter closure gate. Park in the wide areas near the gate, but do not block the main road or any side access (private) roads.

The trail leaves the left side of the parking area near the gate and immediately begins climbing through the dense young forest, switching back a time or two before traversing west into the Heather Creek Valley. The trail climbs steadily alongside the creek, gaining more than 1,000 feet in the 2 miles to the lake. After nearly a mile of climbing, notice how the surrounding forest begins to age. Old, stout trees of massive size are mingled with the young, crowded stands of second-growth fir and

Along the steep trail to Heather Lake

hemlock. At the 1.2-mile mark, the forest is entirely old growth, with ancient hulks towering over the trail and long-dead trunks lying scattered about the forest floor. The decaying fallen trees provide just the rich nourishment seeds need to sprout and grow into young, upstart trees. In this way, the dead trees, or nurse logs, hold the roots of a new generation, closing the circle of forest life. Even buried under snow, these nurse logs are evident. Just look for the long rows of young trees, and imagine them all rooted in one long, straight log.

The trail reaches the Heather Lake Basin at just over 2,400 feet and breaks out of the forest and into open views of the towering summit of Mount Pilchuck beyond. The lake is at a low-enough elevation that at no time should you attempt to cross its ice. The ice is seldom thick enough to support an adult, and even then, it is likely riddled with cracks and fissures which could open and send you into a quick bout of hypothermia.

Campsites can be found around the perimeter of the lake, and the best are on the eastern shore where the slope is most gradual and the view most splendid.

--20--

Lake 22

Rating:	Backcountry
Round trip:	5 miles
Hiking time:	4 hours
Elevation gain:	1,200 feet
High point:	2,440 feet
Best season:	Early January to late February
Maps:	Green Trails: Granite Falls No. 109
Who to contact:	Mount Baker–Snoqualmie National Forest, Darrington Ranger District
	See page 76 for map.

Although the snow is frequently thin at the base of this trail, the route climbs quickly and snowshoes are needed not only for flotation but also for traction on the steep slopes. The workout is extensive, but the rewards are phenomenal. The trail follows a beautiful tumbling creek as it rushes down a narrow gorge. Along the way, the creek drops over no less than four

Icicles and small waterfall along the trail to Lake 22

pretty waterfalls, with each successive one sporting larger and more intricate ice mantles.

To get there, from Granite Falls drive east on Mountain Loop Highway (State Route 530) 1 mile past the Verlot Public Service Center and continue east 2 miles to the Lake 22 Trailhead on the right (south) side of the highway.

If the snow is thin at this low-elevation trailhead, strap your snowshoes on the back of your pack and hike up the trail until the snow deepens. The trail climbs gradually for a quarter mile, then turns straight up the creek valley and rolls through a long series of switchbacks. Frequently, even if the snow isn't deep, snowshoes will be required simply because the beefy crampons on their base afford a sure grip on the slick trail.

The first waterfall is passed a half mile up the trail, and then more are seen at 1 mile, 1.2 miles, and 1.5 miles. Just past the third waterfall, the trail levels out (relatively speaking) as it rolls west along the hillside for several hundred yards before turning back toward the creek. It passes through a couple of these longer, more moderate switchbacks before making a long, straight traverse back to the creek at the fourth falls. From there, it's a quarter-mile climb to the lakeshore.

This trail is steeper and the lake more remote than the nearby Heather Lake route, but it is also less visited in winter months. Some of the open slopes above the trail, especially on the upper reaches, are prone to slide in moderate to high avalanche conditions, so use caution.

--21--

Boardman Lake

Rating:	More difficult
Round trip:	12 miles
Hiking time:	1 to 2 days
Elevation gain:	1,800 feet
High point:	3,000 feet
Best season:	Late December through late February
Maps:	Green Trails: Silverton No. 110
Who to contact:	Mount Baker–Snoqualmie National Forest, Darrington Ranger District

The best way to enjoy this scenic wonderland is by planning to spend the night beside the high mountain lake. By taking at least 2 days to complete the trek, the views and scenery can be enjoyed to their utmost. Making a camp at day's end also means spending several hours in this beautiful area when all the hotshot snowmobilers and speedy skiers are headed for home. Best of all, though, a 2-day trip means watching the sun set in a blaze of midwinter glory and, come morning, watching it rise anew over the orange-dappled peaks of the North Cascades.

To get there, from Granite Falls drive east on the Mountain Loop Highway (State Route 530) 4 miles past the Verlot Public Service Center and turn right (south) into the wide area near the junction with Forest Service Road 4020 (Schweitzer Creek Road). Park here, and start hiking up the heavily visited Schweitzer Creek Road.

Loads of recreationists are usually on the Schweitzer Creek Road system: skiers love it because of the scenic beauty of the area, snowmobilers like it because of the wide roadways and loop possibilities, and snowshoers will love it because of the opportunities to share in the beauty of the area on the gentle trails before leaving the hordes behind and venturing out into the seldom-visited splendor of the narrow trail to the lakes.

To begin the snowshoe trek, walk up the gently climbing Schweitzer Creek Road as it ascends a ridge face above its namesake creek. The road pierces the old, moss-laden forests of the valley bottom and climbs into increasingly young second-growth forest. After 2.5 miles, the scenery picks up and the views increase. The forests give way to open meadows (i.e., clearcuts) that spread like downy white quilts upon the hillside. Beyond these pillowy white meadows stretch the ragged crests of the Mountain Loop peaks: Three Fingers, Big Four, and Vesper Peak all scratch the sky on the far side of the Stillaguamish Valley to the east.

The trail splits at just over 2.5 miles. Stay left on the main road as it rolls east around a small, rounded hilltop. The trail along this section pierces second-growth forests of Douglas fir, with occasional breaks of sunshine as it crosses clearcut meadows. Stay to the edges of the road along here as snowmobilers tend to increase their speed on the long, straight stretches.

Five miles from the parking area at the base of the hill, the trail sweeps right through a hairpin corner. A couple hundred yards past the apex of the turn, find the Boardman Lake Trailhead on the left. This hiking trail climbs gently for just under a mile, passing Lake Evan after a mere 100 yards, before continuing on into increasingly old forest. The trail climbs steadily from Lake Evan but gains just 200 feet along the way. The trail is fairly easy to follow, even in heavy snow years, but if you lose it in the trees, simply head due south, climbing straight up the slope to reach the northern end of Boardman. The trail crosses the lake's outlet stream immediately upon reaching the lake. This area can be a bit tricky because of the jumble of logs clogging the neck of the outlet stream. The debris allows you to keep your feet dry while crossing, but the odd angles of the many logs can make footing precarious at times. Use care when stepping over the logs, and the crossing can be accomplished without undue difficulty. Once across, enjoy the views of the ice-covered lake and distant vistas. To the east, Mallardy Ridge lines the sky. To the north, Boardman Creek leads down into the Stillaguamish Valley, and beyond that are the high peaks of Three Fingers, Big Bear Mountain, and Liberty Mountain. To the south, Bald Mountain rises over the lake basin. Good campsites are located along the eastern shore of the lake for those planning to stay and enjoy the beautiful basin at sunset and sunrise.

To return home, head back down the narrow forest trail to its junction with the road. From there, go right to retrace your steps, or head left and make a loop of the trip. Going this way, the road descends more than a mile, crossing a clearcut and young stands of second-growth timber. About 1.25 miles from the Lake Boardman Trailhead, the road banks right—a blue-diamond blaze on the trees nearby indicates a trail. Continue straight ahead along this connector trail to reach the narrow bed of Forest Service Road No. 4021. Stay right on this new road, and follow it down 2 miles to a junction with Forest Service Road No. 4020. Go left and walk the last 2 miles out to the junction with the Mountain Loop Highway.

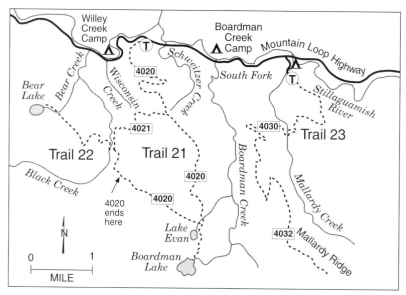

Along the shoreline of Boardman Lake

--22--

Bear Lake

Rating:	More difficult
Round trip:	10 miles
Hiking time:	6 hours
Elevation gain:	1,400 feet
High point:	2,775 feet
Best season:	January through late February
Maps:	Green Trails: Silverton No. 110
Who to contact:	Mount Baker–Snoqualmie National Forest, Darrington Ranger District
	See page 82 for map.

Oddly enough, this trail is largely ignored by skiers and snowmobilers despite its glorious wildernesslike atmosphere and stunning scenery. The trail branches off the Schweitzer Creek Road, which does draw a lot of snow

Snow layered on a downed tree, Bear Lake route

traffic, and climbs gradually to a pretty little alpine lake amid young forest. The route crosses some old clearcut meadows, which provide ample opportunity for snowshoers to bask in the midwinter sun before ducking back under the green canopy of forest that shades most of the route.

The bulk of the climbing is taken care of in the first few miles, leaving a leisurely hike over the last couple miles. That's as it should be because the best views, prettiest forests, and most enjoyable snow lie along the upper sections of the trail. Also, the bottom half of the route is along the Schweitzer Creek Road Loop, which is popular with skiers and snowmobilers.

To get there, from Granite Falls drive east on the Mountain Loop Highway (State Route 530) 4 miles past the Verlot Public Service Center and turn right (south) into the wide area near the junction with Forest Service Road 4020 (Schweitzer Creek Road). Park here, and start hiking up the heavily visited Schweitzer Creek Road.

Expect to share the trail for the first 2.5 miles as it climbs the popular Schweitzer Creek Road. The road ascends a ridge line above the creek. The first half to three-quarters mile of road ambles along a thick rainforest environment—trees heavy with moss and lichen shade the road. But as the route starts to climb the ridge, the forest changes to young second-growth and occasional small clearcuts.

At 2.5 miles, as it crosses the head of Schweitzer Creek, the road splits. This is the start of the Schweitzer Loop—one road eventually leads back to the other. Loopers are best served by going left, but to access Bear Lake, turn right onto Forest Service Road No. 4021 and hike across a generally flat forest and meadow area. The road curves south, providing some nice views east toward Big Four Mountain, Vesper Peak, Sperry Peak, and Little Chief.

Near the 4-mile mark, the road splits again. Most of the ski and snow-mobile tracks will head off on the right fork (Forest Service Road No. 016). Road No. 4021, the left fork, is the road less traveled, but it is also the trail to Bear Lake. So, hooking sharply to the left, cross Black Creek and hike west up a very gentle slope. The road meanders and wanders a bit, but when the snow is heavy (covering the underbrush), straighten out the course by heading cross-country across the neck of the looping turns. Just bear west-northwest, and recross the road in a few hundred yards.

A half mile farther, at 4.5 miles, the road makes a big swing south, and then hooks abruptly northwest. Near the 5-mile mark, a small trail leads due west from the roadway. Hike along this forest path about 200 yards to find Bear Lake at 2,775 feet.

--23--

Mallardy Ridge

Rating: More difficult
Round trip: 10 miles
Hiking time: 6 hours
Elevation gain: 1,900 feet
High point: 3,500 feet
Best season: Late January through early March
Maps: Green Trails: Silverton No. 110
Who to contact: Mount Baker–Snoqualmie National Forest, Darrington Ranger District
See page 82 for map.

Mallardy Ridge is one of the spectacular wild areas that is seldom enjoyed by summer hikers because there are few true trails and no protection from motorized recreationists. Come winter, the old logging roads become de facto trails as the snow drifts over and around them, turning this heavily roaded area into a wild, scenic wonderland. Follow the roads for an easy, care-free outing with the family, or go cross-country to make the journey more difficult and more adventurous. No matter how the ridge is explored, there is plenty of enjoyment for all. In addition to the simple beauty of the snowy playground immediately at hand, the views of the high, craggy peaks of the Mountain Loop Region are astounding. From various points along the snowshoe trails, enjoy views of Three Fingers and White Horse Mountains to the north; Big Four, Sperry, and Vesper Peaks to the east; and Bald Mountain to the south.

Snowshoer heading up the long road to Mallardy Ridge

To get there, from Granite Falls drive east on Mountain Loop Highway (State Route 530) 7.4 miles past the Verlot Public Service Center, and just before crossing the Red Bridge, turn right (south) into the wide parking area near the junction with the Mallardy Ridge Road (Forest Service Road No. 4030).

Snowshoe along the Mallardy Ridge Road as it glides through the ancient cedar forests along the valley bottom. Soon, however, the road tilts upward and begins the long, steady climb up the side of the ridge. If you are looking for a short day trip, consider taking one of the spur roads encountered along the first couple of miles, but bear in mind these side trails lead nowhere (except into pretty snow-painted forests). To make the most of the trek, continue up the main road to the first major road junction at 1.5 miles. Go right onto Forest Service Road No. 4032—the smaller and generally less well-traveled, of the two options—to access Mallardy Ridge. The road rolls up and down for a mile, crossing Mallardy Creek, before the long, southbound ascent of the ridge. The crest is reached at the 5-mile mark and makes an excellent place for a leisurely lunch before turning back.

From the crest, enjoy sweeping views of Bald Mountain—seemingly just an arm's length away, just west of Boardman Creek—as well as the more mammoth hulks of Little Chief Peak to the east and Liberty Mountain to the north.

--24--
Kelcema Lake

Rating:	More difficult
Round trip:	10 miles
Hiking time:	6 hours
Elevation gain:	1,600 feet
High point:	3,182 feet
Best season:	January through February
Maps:	Green Trails: Silverton No. 110
Who to contact:	Mount Baker–Snoqualmie National Forest, Darrington Ranger District

Explore a pretty forest valley and deep lake basin in snowmobile-free splendor since this route is maintained for nonmotorized winter recreation only. The trail is frequented by cross-country skiers, but if snowshoers just think of skiers as fellow snowshoers who prefer long, skinny snowshoes, there is no problem sharing the trail. After all, there is plenty of wonderful country and splendid scenery here for everyone to enjoy. The route follows a small road that parallels Deer Creek on its way up the valley to the Kelcema Lake Trailhead. The route climbs steadily, but at a gentle enough rate that snowshoers of all abilities will enjoy this outing. In addition to a gentle climb, the route offers beautiful old forests to explore, open clearcut meadows to play in, and high craggy ridges and peaks to admire.

To get there, from Granite Falls drive east on Mountain Loop Highway (State Route 530) about 12 miles past the Verlot Public Service Center to the end of the plowed road. Park in the large Sno-Park facility on the north side of the highway.

Find the start of the Deer Creek Road (Forest Service Road No. 4052) near the eastern edge of the parking area and start snowshoeing up the road. The lower section is frequently crowded with families sliding on inner tubes and sleds. Be careful not to trudge across their line of descent as they are more often than not plummeting downhill, out of control. Also, as a matter of courtesy, while trekking up the road, try to avoid stomping down the twin grooves carved by cross-country skis.

As the road climbs through the first, thick grove of second-growth forest, the views are limited to the roadway itself. After just a mile, the road slowly banks west, following the course of the creek, and you can catch a few glimpses north of the crown of Bald Mountain. Gradually, the views increase in quantity and quality. The narrow road continues to roll upstream as the thick second-growth forest gives way first to small clearcuts, and then to older, more mature forests. Near the 2.5-mile mark, stop for a breather and you will find the increasingly pretty views before you are nothing compared to the scenery at your back. Turn around and look down the valley to see a skyline punctuated by Big Four Mountain, and Sperry, Vesper, and Little Chief Peaks.

At 3.5 miles, the trail crosses Deer Creek—stay to the center of the bridge to avoid sloughing snow—and climbs out of the valley bottom. The road gains elevation steeply for the next mile as it sweeps west before switching back to climb toward the headwaters of the creek. At 4.5 miles, the road recrosses the creek and runs into the Kelcema Lake Trailhead. The road continues west for another quarter mile, and most cross-country skiers will follow it out. With wide snowshoes you have a decided advantage over skinny-skis on forest trails, so turn left just after crossing the creek and climb the Kelcema Lake Trail. This narrow path weaves through old second-growth forest—with a few ancient giants left to inspire the younger trees—for a half

The lower section of the trail to Kelcema Lake

mile. The trail climbs gently along this stretch, and because the trail corridor is fairly wide, the route is easy to follow. The lake is met near the outlet stream, and some nice campsites are scattered along its shores as well as plenty of places to sit and enjoy a quiet lunch while soaking in the beauty of the region. Bald Mountain, to the south, towers over the lake basin, and Devils Peak is visible across the valley to the east.

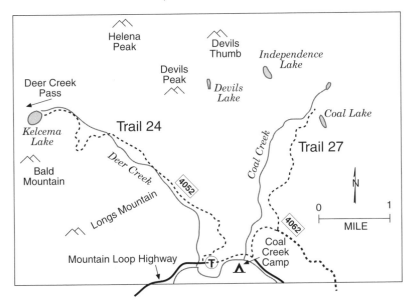

--25--

Marten Creek

Rating:	Backcountry
Round trip:	6.6 miles
Hiking time:	5 hours
Elevation gain:	1,300 feet
High point:	2,800 feet
Best season:	Late December through early February
Maps:	Green Trails: Silverton No. 110
Who to contact:	Mount Baker–Snoqualmie National Forest, Darrington Ranger District

Marten Creek Trail is an oft-overlooked route in summer months that is virtually forgotten come winter. That is a blessing to those who know of, and take advantage of, the beauty of this secluded little forest valley. The crowds skip over this trail because there are no high, wind-swept ridges to explore and no deep alpine lake basins in which to camp. But there is a narrow, winding trail that is loads of fun to follow on snowshoes, a rich forest ecosystem to explore, and a host of wildlife to view and appreciate.

(In low-snow years, it may be necessary to carry the snowshoes on the lower section of trail, but the upper valley is generally deep in snow by mid-December.)

To get there, from Granite Falls drive east on the Mountain Loop Highway about 9 miles past the Verlot Public Service Center, and just past Marten Creek Campground (closed in winter), turn around and park in the narrow parking area on the left (north) side of the highway at the Marten Creek Trailhead.

The trail climbs steadily from the highway, staying well above the creek itself for the first mile. The views are limited to the local forest scenery, but that is rich enough to hold anyone's attention. Of course, there's not a lot of time for gawking as this narrow, under-maintained trail is rough and, with a blanket of snow on it, avoiding snowshoe-tearing branches and toe-grabbing logs requires undivided attention at times.

At other times, however, the trail is open and easily followed. These stretches—especially past the 1-mile mark—are where the views can be best appreciated. After the initial 1.5 miles, the trail stops climbing and rolls into a long traverse of the ridge wall above the creek, dipping at times to water level before angling back up into the open forest of above. Around 2.5 miles, the trail angles left toward the head of the valley. It continues another mile before the formal trail peters out. It's possible, when the snow is stable, to continue up the valley for another half mile to get right under the shadow of the near-vertical headwall. Just don't get too close as avalanches aren't the only danger here. Rockfalls are much more common than snowslides, and just as deadly. If the weather is warming, or the avalanche danger is moderate or great, don't push past the end of the formal trail.

Because the creek valley is relatively wide-bottomed with plenty of lush undergrowth for forage, it's common for deer to be found in this area.

Small mammal tracks in snow

And where there are deer, there are cougars. Count yourself lucky if you see one of these big, elusive cats. Usually the only proof that mountain lions exist in these woods comes in the form of deep, clawless tracks pressed into the snow.

Big animals aren't the only inhabitants here. Grouse roost in the trees near the creek, snowshoe hares scamper through the underbrush along the trail, and at least one great-horned owl glides silently between the trees looking for a midwinter meal of rabbit, vole, or marten. Yes, the creek is aptly named—martens have also been seen along this pretty trail.

--26--
Big Four Ice Caves Viewpoint

Rating: Easiest
Round trip: 6 miles
Hiking time: 3.5 hours
Elevation gain: 250 feet
High point: 1,800 feet
Best season: January through March
Maps: Green Trails: Silverton No. 110
Who to contact: Mount Baker–Snoqualmie National Forest, Darrington Ranger District

Want a walk through a gorgeous winter wonderland without a sweaty climb up a steep trail? This route offers all the beauty and majesty found in the wintry mountains without the strenuous workout usually required to see such splendor. It is the perfect trail for taking the family on a gentle snowshoe stroll or for introducing newbies to the joys of snowshoeing.

The trail is wide—actually, most of the "trail" is on a section of the unplowed Mountain Loop Highway—and flat, so first-timers can get the feel for walking on snowshoes without having to worry about climbing, crossing, or descending steep slopes. But despite its mild nature, this trail accesses some truly wild country. Trekking up to the base of Big Four, snowshoers can gawk in awe at the towering mountain before them. The granite monolith of Big Four Mountain, with its long icicle fingers and snowy cap, captivates most visitors, but it's not the only natural wonder found here. Huge ancient trees, a clear, ice-rimmed river, and hordes of animals—big and small—are here to enjoy as well.

Icicles dangling off a tree branch are evidence of the freeze-and-thaw cycle typical of low elevation areas.

To get there, from Granite Falls drive east on the Mountain Loop Highway (State Route 530) about 12 miles past the Verlot Public Service Center to the end of the plowed road. Park in the large Sno-Park facility on the north side of the highway.

Leave the parking area, and trek up the snowbound Mountain Loop Highway as it follows the Stillaguamish River upstream. The road is lined with towering cedar and fir trees—many of which sport long, flowing beards of green. At a half mile, cross the sparkling waters of Coal Creek as it rushes in from the north to empty into the Stillaguamish River. Follow the road more than 2 miles until a small side road veers away to the right. This is the entrance to the Big Four Picnic Area and the trailhead for the Big Four Ice Caves Trail.

The ice caves themselves are typically blocked by early December—heavy snowfall and continual avalanches keep the caves capped tight throughout the winter—but the 1-mile trail from the picnic area is worth exploring. The trail leads to the base of Big Four and, along the way, offers outstanding views of the giant rock face of the mountain. Though it may be tempting to snowshoe right up to the jumbled pile of snow at the mouth of the ice caves, resist that temptation. That pile of snowballs is what remains of the devastating avalanches that flash down the side of the mountain after every snowstorm and after most sunny mornings. The bright sun on the rock face weakens the snow and ice, sending it crashing down on the trail below with no absolutely no warning.

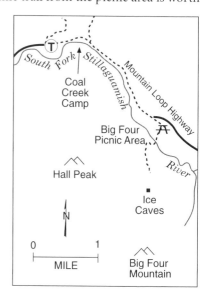

--27--

Coal Creek

Rating:	More difficult
Round trip:	6.5 miles
Hiking time:	4 hours
Elevation gain:	900 feet
High point:	2,400 feet
Best season:	January through March
Maps:	Green Trails: Silverton No. 110
Who to contact:	Mount Baker–Snoqualmie National Forest, Darrington Ranger District
	See page 89 for map.

The snow-covered sections of the Mountain Loop Highway are open to anyone and everyone with the means to enjoy the snow—be it cross-country skis, snowshoes, inner tubes, dogsleds, or snowmobiles—but the side valleys leading away from the main road are often ignored by all of them. That's a mistake that snowshoers can quietly take advantage of. The Coal Creek Valley is the first large valley leading north away from the Mountain Loop Highway, and it offers outstanding opportunities to trek through untouched meadows, open stands of forest, and along clear, sparkling creeks. There is no true trail much of the way, but the wide valley allows snowshoers to pick out their own paths while enjoying the quiet basin and its surrounding natural beauty.

To get there, from Granite Falls drive east on the Mountain Loop Highway (State Route 530) about 12 miles past the Verlot Public Service Center to the end of the plowed road. Park in the large Sno-Park facility on the north side of the highway.

From the parking area, follow the Mountain Loop Highway up the Stillaguamish River Valley for nearly a mile. Look for the Coal Creek Campground on the right. Just past the campground, cross Coal Creek, and then bear left onto a tiny spur that leads north. This road ends in just a few

Jay in the trees alongside the trail to Coal Lake

hundred yards, but a faint skier and snowshoer trail—marked with blue-diamond blazes—climbs up the Coal Creek Valley. The trail pierces a stand of old second-growth forest. The blazes, sporadically placed, are sometimes difficult to see. If the next blaze is out of sight, just continue a gentle climb, going straight up the face of the thinly forested hill while staying well above the creek itself. In less than a mile, the trail encounters Forest Service Road No. 4062. Turn left and follow it as it traverses, and gently climbs, the valley wall on the east side of Coal Creek. The road ends in another mile, offering picturesque views down the valley to the Stillaguamish River Valley and beyond to Hall and Marble Peaks.

--*28*--
Silver Star View

Rating:	More difficult
Round trip:	4 to 20 miles
Hiking time:	3 hours to 2 days
Elevation gain:	700 feet
High point:	3,500 feet
Best season:	December through early March
Maps:	Green Trails: Washington Pass No. 50 and Mazama No. 51
Who to contact:	Okanogan National Forest, Methow Valley Ranger District, Winthrop Office

This route provides the unique opportunity to snowshoe up the middle of one of the most popular highways in the state. Come summer, State Route 20—the North Cascades Highway—is swarming with tourist traffic. But by December the road is snowbound, and it stays that way until June or July most years. That means snowshoers and cross-country skiers can play in the road without fear. Of course, there is still a danger of being run over, but the danger comes not from cars and trucks but from sliding snow. Avalanche chutes line the upper section of the highway as it approaches Washington Pass, so recreationists are well advised to stick to the lower areas and avoid the route altogether when avalanche dangers are moderate or higher.

One of the views from the Silver Star route

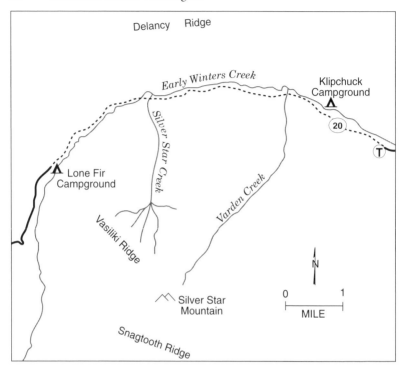

To get there, from Winthrop drive west on State Route 20 to the end of the plowed road. Park in the wide parking area.

Strap on your snowshoes, and trek up the highway, staying to the side of the road to avoid tromping on skiers' tracks and to avoid collisions with snowmobilers who occasional zip along this route. The road parallels the Methow River up-valley and offers great views of the many high peaks that mark the crest of the North Cascades. The road makes a long, gradual curve to the left. Snowshoeing up the first 2 miles, the view is straight ahead toward the Needles—a collage of rocky spires towering up to 8,140 feet. As the road curves to the southwest, the magnificent crown of Silver Star Mountain comes into view on the left, directly above the road. As beautiful as this mountain is, it is also highly dangerous. Many of the avalanches that keep the road unplowable (and therefore open only to snow recreationists) are spawned on Silver Star.

Just past the Silver Star Creek crossing, around 6 miles, all the

Washington Pass peaks are visible on clear days. With Silver Star Mountain on the left and the Needles on the right, look for Tower Mountain, Cutthroat Peak, Whistler Mountain, and Liberty Bell Mountain (partially obscured by Silver Star) in between.

Because of the risk of avalanches caused by changing conditions, overnight camping is discouraged. For a quiet day outing, snowshoe up the road until lunch time, and then return home. Speedsters might work their way up the valley as far as Lone Fir Campground, but that makes a long day—it is more than 10 miles beyond the end of the plowed road.

--29--
Upper River Run

Rating:	Easiest
Round trip:	6 miles
Hiking time:	4 hours
Elevation gain:	500 feet
High point:	2,800 feet
Best season:	December through early March
Maps:	Green Trails: Mazama No. 51
Who to contact:	Okanogan National Forest, Methow Valley Ranger District, Winthrop Office

Nothing beats an easy snowshoe stroll through the world-renowned winter wonderland of the Methow Valley. Rolling meadows of snow, nestled amid the tall, willowy aspen trees, sturdy pines, and towering firs, offer a wonderful playground for snowshoers, and the River Run Trail system is the way to experience these wonders.

Although created with cross-country skiers in mind, the flat trails alongside the Methow River are just as enjoyable for snowshoers. They can hike along and soak in the beautiful scenery around the trail, and exult in the inspiring views of high ridges and towering peaks that surround the valley. From young kids to seasoned veterans, snowshoers of all abilities will enjoy the easy trails of River Run.

Because these trails are heavily used by skiers, snowshoers will be asked—sometimes told—to stay to the extreme edges of the trails, and when possible, to stay off the groomed track completely. Also, the trails cross private property occasionally, so visitors shouldn't wander far from the actual trail corridors.

To get there, from Winthrop drive west on State Route 20 to Mazama and continue another mile before turning left (south) into the Early Winters/Arrowleaf property. Stay left, and follow the signs to Jacks Cabin a quarter mile down the road. (If you reach the Freestone Inn at the end of the half mile road, you've gone too far.) Purchase a trail pass at Jacks Cabin.

Hike west from the parking areas, passing Freestone Inn and, in a quarter mile, several small cabins—the original Early Winters Cabins—alongside Early Winters Creek. Angle toward the highway, and cross the creek via the State Route 20 bridge. Then cross the highway, and pick up the trail system on the north side of the road. The trail turns right and leads away from the highway. A few hundred yards later, it veers left and follows the Methow River upstream. In the next half mile, several trail junctions are passed—one leads right, crosses the river, and ends at the North Cascades Basecamp property. Others merely cross meadows and create an intricate network of loops. The trails extend about 3.5 miles upstream from the highway crossing, for a trip of more than 7 miles. But shorter trips can be had by making use of the many connectors and cut-off trails.

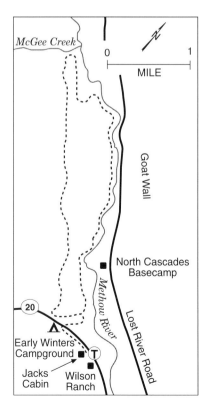

A full loop is best done by sticking to the River Run Trail as it follows the river upstream. At the upper end of the route, stay left and cross the wide valley bottom to access Jacks Trail at the base of the western valley wall. Return to Jacks Cabin via this trail.

By late October, while the aspens are still decked out in gold, there is often enough snow for snowshoeing along this route

--*30*--
Cedar Falls

Rating:	More difficult
Round trip:	7.6 miles
Hiking time:	5 hours
Elevation gain:	800 feet
High point:	3,600 feet
Best season:	December through early March
Maps:	Green Trails: Mazama No. 51
Who to contact:	Okanogan National Forest, Methow Valley Ranger District, Winthrop Office

This trail represents one of the best chances for snowshoers to escape the ever-present hordes of skiers who clog the tracks and trails of the Methow Valley. While the occasional skier may struggle up the narrow trail, the route is mostly ignored simply because so many other trails are better suited to their long skis. Snowshoes, though, make easy work of this trail, climbing gently as it does through deep, dry-side forests.

Massive ponderosa pine, aspens, larch, cedar, and fir all fill this valley and provide habitat to an array of birds and animals. Chittering, begging camp-robber jays flit through the limbs, woodpeckers hammer on the trunks, and grouse and ptarmigan scurry around the roots of the big trees. Great-horned owls are frequently seen hunting in this valley, which has plenty of prey animals for them to consume. Aside from the grouse and ptarmigan, the owls feast on the resident martens, weasels, mice, chipmunks, squirrels, and other small mammals.

The trail ends at the site of a pretty little waterfall. This cascade is rather unspectacular in summer months, but cloaked in snow and ice, the falls becomes a wonderful work of water art.

To get there, from Winthrop drive west on State Route 20 to the Early Winters Campground. Continue west 2.3 miles to find Forest Service Road No. 200 on the left. Park in the wide space (room for only one or two cars most of the time) at the base of this road, staying well clear of the traffic lanes of State Route 20.

The hike begins with a gentle snowshoe walk up Road No. 200 to its end, about 1 mile up the valley. At that point, the true trail begins. It is a

The lower section of Cedar Creek

narrow hikers' path following the valley wall high above Cedar Creek. The trail is easy to follow even in heavy snow, although it is slow going at times as the route weaves up and down, in and out of tree wells. At 2.5 miles out, the trail angles down toward the creek and the last mile is right alongside the waterway. Views are limited, although periodic peeks open up of Sandy Butte to the east, and Driveway Butte can be seen to the north (best viewed on the return trip when facing north) from the lower sections of the trail.

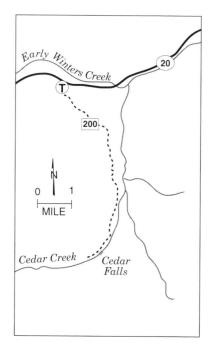

At 3.8 miles, find a nice view of Cedar Falls, a small cascade on this little creek. The icy crust and snowy mantle that surround the falls give it a fairy-tale appearance that is worthy of a photo or two before returning home.

--31--
Paul Mountain

Rating:	Easiest to more difficult
Round trip:	7 miles
Hiking time:	5 hours
Elevation gain:	1,500 feet
High point:	3,600 feet
Best season:	January through early March
Maps:	Green Trails: Doe Mountain No. 52
Who to contact:	Okanogan National Forest, Methow Valley Ranger District, Winthrop Office

This is a trek that can be tailored to any snowshoer: from an easy, flat walk perfect for families and first-time 'shoers to a strenuous climb along a well-graded road for more adventurous sorts or to a full-on snowshoe scramble to the top of a gnarly peak for snowshoe mountaineers.

Generally, the best bet is to stick with the initial riverside walk, and maybe add a short snowshoe up the flank of the mountain to attain a better view of the glorious valley below. Leave the mountaineering to those fanatics who use snowshoes merely as tools to get to the top rather than as a specific form of recreation separate and complete in itself.

The gentle road walk provides excellent opportunities to see and experience the snowy ponderosa pine forests that line the beautiful Eightmile Creek. Along the way, and from the trail climbing the flank of Paul Mountain, there are stunning views of Buck Mountain (not the same Buck Mountain as mentioned in Route 32) and Paul Mountain itself.

To get there, from Winthrop leave the north end of town on East Chewuch River Road, and nearly 7 miles out of town, turn left across the river and then go right onto the West Chewuch River Road (Forest Service

Snow-covered trees along the trail to Paul Mountain

Road 51) as it continues north. About 2.6 miles after crossing the river, turn left into the Sno-Park at the base of Eight-mile Road.

Many snowshoeing options are available upon leaving this Sno-Park, but for this trail, head straight up the wide track of Eight-mile Road. This route follows the pretty, tumbling waters of Eight-mile Creek and provides countless opportunities to walk along its edge and listen to the gentle music of its water splashing over ice-crusted rocks. Generally in midwinter, several arching snow-bridges span the small creek. As tempting as it may be to point your snowshoes across one of these, resist that urge, as the delicate bridges seldom are strong enough to bear the weight of a small animal, let alone a plodding snowshoer.

As the road approaches Flat Campground at 2 miles, it crosses the one truly safe bridge—one made of iron and wood—over the creek. Now on the north side of the creek, wander through Flat Camp, enjoying the views of Paul Mountain and the long crest of Eight-mile Ridge that leads north away from the peak's summit.

To find a better view of Eight-mile Valley, follow the road a few hundred yards farther up the valley to a small road leading off to the right. This route climbs steeply up the flank of Paul Mountain, and as it passes through increasingly thin forests, it offers many views along the length of Eight-mile Valley and across it to Buck Mountain (4,490 feet). The road continues for nearly 2 miles before it divides into a maze of spur roads, but from the first of these multiple road junctions at 3,160 feet, the views are remarkable. With Paul Mountain towering overhead, the pretty ribbon of Eight-mile Creek lies in the bottom of the deep valley spread out at your feet.

--32--

Buck Mountain

Rating: More difficult
Round trip: 8.5 miles
Hiking time: 6.5 hours
Elevation gain: 2,500 feet
High point: 6,100 feet
Best season: December through early March
Maps: Green Trails: Loup Loup No. 85
Who to contact: Okanogan National Forest, Methow Valley Ranger District, Twisp Office

The Okanogan National Forest seems to have more fire watchtowers still standing than any other national forest in the state. The Buck Mountain Lookout is one of them, and like many of the other towers in the Methow Valley region, Buck Mountain's lookout makes an excellent destination for winter recreationists. Not only are outstanding views to be had from the lookout-clad summit of the mountain, but the local scenery on the way up the side of the peak is stunning in its own right.

Wildlife is also present along this quiet trail, and even when the animals are out of sight, their tracks give away their recent passing. Look for snowshoe hares, ptarmigans, and an array of birds flitting to and fro through the forest. This area is also home to bobcats, cougars, and coyotes and is well within the range of the tiny population of wolves living a precarious life in the North Cascades. (Although the odds of seeing one of these majestic pack animals are extreme, just knowing they may hunt these hills is enough to give the region a special wild feel.)

If there is any question about the abundance of wildlife throughout this region, just consider the names of the hills and mountains that occupy the glorious views from Buck Mountain. (Yes, herds of deer—both mule deer and whitetails—browse the flanks of this peak, with many males, or bucks, in their ranks.) Bobcat Mountain sits beside Beaver Mountain to the northwest. Bear Mountain anchors the end of Coyote Ridge to the southwest, and Salmon Creek Valley is a dark cut in the hills to the northeast.

To get there, from Twisp drive east on State Route 20 to the summit of Loup Loup Pass and continue another 2.5 miles east to a junction with Buck Mountain Road on the left (north). Park in the plowed pullout at the base of Buck Mountain Road.

As you hike up Buck Mountain Road, you are likely to find plenty of cross-country ski tracks along the way. Try to avoid stepping on the primary ski tracks—those that look to have been used the most—whenever possible, and there is no reason snowshoers and skiers can't enjoy the trail together.

The road climbs steadily, but not too steeply, for nearly 2 miles, passing several poorly marked side roads along the way. Stay on the main trail, which rolls due north until hitting a tight switchback at 2 miles followed by a long, looping curve back to the north. Once through this curve, which circles around the flank of a pretty, unnamed peak (4,573 feet), the trail bears northwest. At 3 miles, the top of a long ridge is reached. From here, the road weaves and wanders around the contours of the land as it bears northeast toward the top of Buck Mountain. You can forgo much of that roundabout navigation by using the tightly shuttered lookout cabin at the summit that is visible along the open ridge. Simply follow the path of least resistance toward that building, and shave as much as a mile off the road distance.

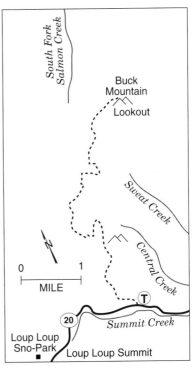

Depending on the winds, some dangerous corniced drifts may have built up along the top of the ridge. Generally, the east side of the ridge crest is the safest for snowshoeing, but the conditions will have to be evaluated during the hike.

The last few hundred feet involve a rather steep climb straight up to the lookout tower. This is worth the exertion because the narrow summit offers spectacular views in every direction. On clear days, gaze north into Canada, east in the Columbia Basin, west to the jagged crest of the North Cascades, and south over the Sawtooth Wilderness Area.

Coyote tracks parallel those of snowshoers, Buck Mountain route

--𝄞𝄞--

Lookout Mountain

Rating:	More difficult
Round trip:	8 miles
Hiking time:	5 hours
Elevation gain:	2,100 feet
High point:	5,500 feet
Best season:	December through early March
Maps:	Green Trails: Twisp No. 84
Who to contact:	Okanogan National Forest, Methow Valley Ranger District, Twisp Office

This is one of the classic snow routes in an area famous for nonmotorized winter recreation. The Methow Valley has long been recognized as a mecca for cross-country fanatics, but snowshoers will find the hills and valleys of this thinly forested mountain region just as much fun.

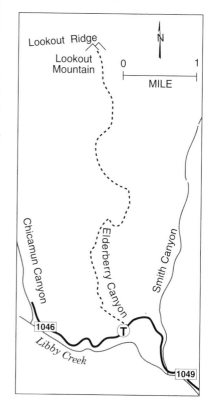

The Lookout Mountain route combines a modest warm-up hike up a narrow access road and a long cross-country climb along the open steppes of a wind-swept flank of Lookout Mountain. The route provides plenty of local scenery to admire and enjoy, but the real thrill is found on the upper slopes, where sweeping views encompass the majority of the Okanogan National Forest. Gaze out over the ragged crest of the Sawtooth Range to the south, admire the view of the expansive Twisp River and Methow River Valleys, and stare in awe at the shimmering white peaks of the Cascade Crest to the west.

To get there, from Twisp drive south on State Route 153 to Carlson

Along the road below Lookout Mountain

and continue another mile before turning right (west) onto Libby Creek Road (Forest Service Road No. 1049). Stay right at the first road junction, at 2.5 miles, and then, at 3.6 miles, turn left onto Forest Service Road No. 1046. Drive a half mile on this road, and park at the small unofficial snow park area at the base of Forest Service Road No. 200 on the left.

The first 1.5 miles follow Road No. 200 as it climbs the west side of Elderberry Canyon toward the summit of Lookout Mountain. The ascent along this section is gradual, gaining just over 1,000 feet in that distance. As the road crosses the creek and starts to climb the opposite valley wall, the going gets tougher. For the easiest approach, stick to the road as it loops south a half mile before switching back and climbing north to reach the ridge top.

Because the trees are thin from here on out, if you are feeling adventurous, leave the road to the skiers and put your snowshoe cleats to the test by angling up the valley wall at a steeper angle, crossing the road somewhere after it has started back from the long loop south. This will shave more than a half mile off the hiking distance, but it will put a burn in your thighs. Take a breather after you rejoin the road and enjoy the increasingly spectacular views. To the south, the Sawtooths are rising into view and north, straight up the ridge line, the small elevated wooden cabin at the summit of Lookout Mountain beckons.

Take a visual bearing off the lookout cabin, and lay in a course to intercept it. The upper ridge is open meadow and generally easy going. Nearly 1.5 miles separate the upper end of the road and the lookout structure, but the slope is only moderately steep and the snow is generally well-packed by the breezes that continually caress this peak.

The lookout tower is boarded up for winter—no need to watch for fires when the forests are wrapped in a protective cocoon of snow—but you can enjoy a well-deserved snack on the leeward side of the building while soaking in the world-famous winter scenery of the sprawling Methow Valley.

--34--
Eagle Creek

Rating:	Backcountry
Round trip:	5 to 18 miles
Hiking time:	4 hours to 2 days
Elevation gain:	Up to 4,900 feet
High point:	7,300 feet
Best season:	January through early March
Maps:	Green Trails: Buttermilk Butte No. 83
Who to contact:	Okanogan National Forest, Methow Valley Ranger District, Twisp Office

Although this route is recommended as a day hike, snowshoers with advanced skills and winter savvy may use this trail as the launching pad for adventures of several days in the wild, wonderful Sawtooth Wilderness Area.

Eagle Creek Trail rolls around the flanks of Duckbill Mountain and beyond to Eagle Pass in the shadow of Battle Mountain on the crest of the Sawtooth Range.

But most snowshoers won't get that far. Instead, snowshoe up the steadily climbing Eagle Creek Valley for 3 or 4 miles for pretty views of Duckbill Mountain and out across the Twisp River Valley to Canyon Creek Ridge. The trail pierces sun-dappled old-growth pine forests and climbs alongside a sparkling mountain stream. This route is virtually ignored when blanketed in snow, so snowshoers are almost assured of solitude in this winter paradise.

To get there, from Twisp drive 14 miles west on the Twisp River Road (Forest Service Road No. 44) to War Creek Campground. Continue for a quarter mile past War Creek Camp, and turn left onto a small road leading across a bridge spanning the Twisp River. After crossing the river, turn left onto Forest Service Road No. 4420 and drive 1 mile to the base of a small

Snow pillows on the rocks of Eagle Creek

spur road, Forest Service Road No. 080, on the right. Park here. At times, the end of the plowed road will be at the bridge above War Creek. If that is the case, park in the wide plowed-out parking area at the end of the road and walk the mile to Road No. 080.

As you snowshoe up Road No. 080, pause at times to turn and look back at the wide Twisp River Valley and the towering wall of Canyon Creek Ridge above it. The road angles west, and then switches back to the east to end at the Eagle Creek Trailhead after just 1 mile. The trail then climbs alongside Eagle Creek, almost immediately weaving through a mini-course of switchbacks before entering a long, climbing run up the valley. The trail is generally easy to spot, even in heavy snow, as it boasts a wide corridor through the thin old forest. Watch for wildlife along the creek—birds and small mammals frequently scurry around the trail.

At 2.5 miles, the trail forks (3,800 feet). This is an excellent place to pause for lunch, enjoy a leisurely exploration of the local flora, and then turn back.

If you want to put a few more miles under your snowshoes, you must make a decision. The left fork climbs a steep series of switchbacks to gain a high bench on the flank of Duckbill Mountain. It then traverses east to follow Oval Creek upstream into the Lake Chelan-Sawtooth Wilderness. The right fork is the preferred route. It loops through a single switchback, and then continues upstream along Eagle Creek.

After another 4 miles, near mile 6.5, the trail hooks right and climbs steeply toward the ridge at the head of the wall. At 8.3 miles, the trail crests the ridge at Eagle Pass (7,300 feet). Getting to this point requires winter mountaineering skills and advanced avalanche-recognition skills.

--*35*--

East Fork Foss River

Rating:	More difficult
Round trip:	14 miles
Hiking time:	1 to 2 days
Elevation gain:	1,400 feet
High point:	3,000 feet
Best season:	Late December through early April
Maps:	Green Trails: Skykomish No. 175 and Stevens Pass No. 176
Who to contact:	Mount Baker–Snoqualmie National Forest, Skykomish Ranger District
	See page 118 for map.

Here's a route that lets snowshoers push themselves to the limit of their endurance, or if they'd rather, lets them enjoy a wonderful wilderness trek without much effort. The trail weaves through beautiful old-growth forest along the bottom of a wide river valley for much of its length before turning near-vertical to climb into a high alpine lakes basin. Those looking for a gentle stretch of the legs and a quiet snowy camp can call it a day at the bottom of the steep climb, while the "no pain, no gain" crowd can muscle their way up the slick slopes and right to the edge of the lakes before pitching camp for a well-deserved rest. Either way, enjoy wonderful scenery, stunning views, and a quiet solitude seldom experienced in the popular Alpine Lakes Wilderness.

To get there, from Everett drive east on US 2 toward Stevens Pass. After passing the Skykomish Ranger Station on the left, continue another half mile and turn right (south) onto the Foss River Road (Forest Service Road No. 68). Follow this road nearly 2 miles to the end of the plowed road and a wide parking area at 1,300-feet elevation.

Snowshoe up the road as it gently climbs alongside the Foss River. The first mile is a multiple-use winter recreation area, so expect to see, or maybe just hear, snowmobiles along this section. But once past the Tonga Ridge Road junction, the route is reserved for nonmotorized recreation, so plan on peace and quiet for the remainder of the journey.

At 1.8 miles from the parking lot, leave the wide roadway by climbing off the left side of the road onto the Foss River Trail. This narrow wilderness path follows the east bank of the East Fork Foss River for 5 miles. The

Looking up the Foss River Valley

trail is generally easy to follow. It was, in fact, once the route of a narrow-gauge railroad that steamed up and down the valley hauling ore out of mine claims and supplies up to the hardrock miners. The trail is fairly flat and gentle, making easy going for snowshoers of all abilities. But it's not all just boring trail walking. Along this stretch of trail there are countless opportunities for you to dip down into riverside meadows to explore the snowy landscape and the water's edge—just be careful not to get too close to the river's edge.

The river valley is wide and beautiful with enough openings in the old-growth forest to allow views up toward the jagged peaks of the

Alpine Lakes Wilderness. Bald Eagle Peak towers over the western valley wall while glacier-studded Mount Daniel fills the sky to the southeast. Look straight up the valley to see the 7,899-foot mountain as well as its neighbor, 7,492-foot Mount Hinman.

Numerous fine campsites are all along this stretch of the trail, but the best are in the broad riverside meadows about 5 miles from your car, and again at 6.8 miles, where the trail suddenly veers west away from the river and climbs steeply into the high lakes basin of Necklace Valley. This corner near the river, with good views all around, and good selection of campsites in the surrounding forest, is the end of the road for all but the most fanatic snowshoers.

If you want to push your skills and endurance to the limits, and if the avalanche danger is low, struggle up the last 2.5 miles of trail as it climbs some 2,200 feet to reach the lower lakes in the Necklace chain. The payoff is great, with the wide lakes basin, deep snow-bowls, and awesome views of the major Alpine Lakes Peaks. However, the expense is extreme physical exertion in an area highly prone to avalanche danger.

It's much more enjoyable to skip the last leg of the trail and simply bask in the glorious beauty of the winter wilderness environment of the East Fork Foss River. Save the high alpine lakes for summer hikes.

--36--
Tonga Ridge

Rating:	Easiest
Round trip:	7 miles
Hiking time:	5 hours
Elevation gain:	1,400 feet
High point:	5,100 feet
Best season:	November through December
Maps:	Green Trails: Skykomish No. 175 and Stevens Pass No. 176
Who to contact:	Mount Baker–Snoqualmie National Forest, Skykomish Ranger District

This could be one of the best early-season snowshoe routes in the state. Ideally, visit this area when the snow is thin enough down low so that the road is passable to cars but the trail itself has enough snow to make snowshoes

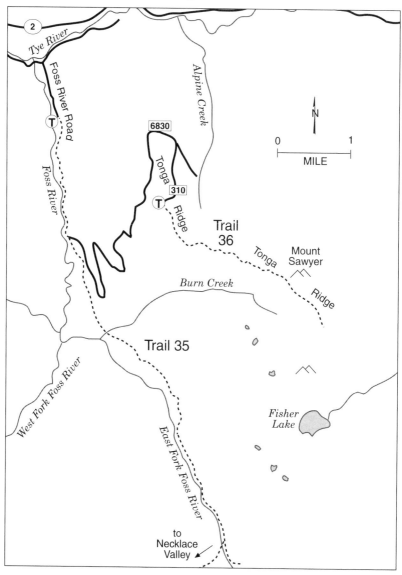

worthwhile. Mid to late November is usually the time to find those conditions. Visit then and the trail will be uncrowded, the views unbelievable, and the memories unforgettable. By late December, however, the access road is blocked by snow and clogged with snowmobiles and weekend skiers. The route will be packed by the "multi-use" crowds until late spring when the road melts out, but the trail retains its blanket of snow. Come back then for one last hurrah on snowshoes before breaking out the hiking boots.

Heavily laden trees along the Tonga Ridge route

To get there, from Everett drive east on US 2 toward Stevens Pass. After passing the Skykomish Ranger Station, which will be on the left, continue another half mile and turn right (south) onto the Foss River Road (Forest Service Road No. 68). Follow this road 3 miles to the junction with Forest Service Road No. 6830, and turn left (east) onto Road No. 6830. Climb 3.3 miles up this road to the top of the ridge and a junction with a small spur road, Forest Service Road No. 310. Turn right onto Road No. 310, and continue to the snow line or the end of the road (1.5 miles) at 4,400 feet.

The Tonga Ridge Trail begins at the end of Road No. 310. From the trailhead, the narrow trail climbs modestly for a mile, gaining just 500 feet, as it heads to the crest of Tonga Ridge proper. The initial leg of the trail skirts an old clearcut before entering thick second-growth forest. That in turn, gives way to old growth and periodic meadows along the ridge top. The trail rolls along just under the crest of the ridge for a total of 3 miles, passing under the high crown of Mount Sawyer before cresting at 4,800 feet in Sawyer Pass.

If you're feeling adventurous, climb south from the pass and take a hard-to-follow trail through the trees to the crest of an unnamed knoll (5,100 feet) before dropping down to Fisher Lake, some 2 miles distant from Sawyer Pass. A better plan, however, is to hunker down at the pass for a leisurely lunch while committing the outstanding vistas to memory. Terrace Mountain lurks to the south, providing a pretty foreground to the high, glacier-studded summits of Mount Daniel and Mount Hinman beyond. To the north, Mount Sawyer lines the afternoon sky. To the east are the high peaks of the Cascade Crest: Surprise Mountain, Spark Plug Mountain, and Mac Peak among them. To the west is the deep cut of the Foss River Valley.

-- 37 --

Lake Susan Jane

Rating:	Most difficult
Round trip:	7 miles
Hiking time:	3.5 hours
Elevation gain:	1,200 feet
High point:	5,200 feet
Best season:	December through early April
Maps:	Green Trails: Stevens Pass No. 176
Who to contact:	Mount Baker–Snoqualmie National Forest, Skykomish Ranger District

Few sections of the Pacific Crest Trail can be enjoyed in midwinter, but this is one of them. The trail leads from a crowded ski area to a tiny wilderness lake amid a snow-blanketed forest. Snowshoers can amuse themselves watching

Tree in disguise near the shores of Lake Susan Jane

the out-of-control antics of downhill skiers and snowboarders on the first mile of the hike and then put those crowds behind them and enjoy a quiet day amid wildlife of a different sort—whiskey jacks, snowshoe hares, snowy white ptarmigans (large, ground-roosting birds), martens, and even an occasional fox may be seen darting through the drifts.

To get there, from Everett drive east on US 2 to the summit of Stevens Pass. Park in the ski area parking lots on the south side of the highway.

Before strapping on the snowshoes, walk up the slope past the ski lodge and angle off to the left to get clear of the downhill ski runs. The Pacific Crest Trail actually slices diagonally across the ski area, but snowshoeing on groomed ski runs is frowned upon. So stay on the outside edge of the ski runs on the left, and climb up along the border of the ski area. As the ski runs taper south to merge at the top of the Tye Chairlift, veer southwest, still skirting the downhill runs, to traverse along a wide bench at the base of a steep hillside. Continue to climb, slanting off to the right, until the top of the ridge is reached in about 1.5 miles (5,200 feet). Turning south, drop off the back side of the ridge to skirt around the headwall of Mill Creek Valley, and pass under the high tension powerlines that carry electricity from the upper Columbia River dams across Stevens Pass to the Puget Sound area.

The Pacific Crest Trail drops steeply downslope, looping through a few switchbacks. Most winter recreationists find it easier to just angle down and across the slope. Continue almost due south, staying above the 4,500-foot level on the eastern flank of the ridge that is the Cascade Crest. An old road is passed at about 2.5 miles, and Lake Susan Jane—a small pond set in a quiet forest glade—is reached at 3.5 miles.

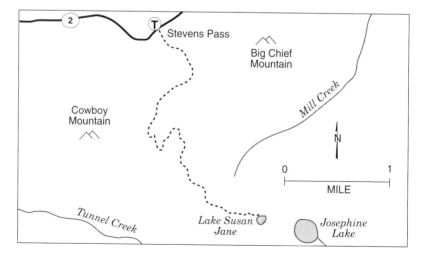

-- 38 --
Skyline Lake

Rating:	More difficult
Round trip:	3 miles
Hiking time:	2 hours
Elevation gain:	1,200 feet
High point:	5,200 feet
Best season:	December through early April
Maps:	Green Trails: Benchmark Mountain No. 144 and Stevens Pass No. 176
Who to contact:	Mount Baker–Snoqualmie National Forest, Skykomish Ranger District

A short but strenuous climb to a high alpine lake, buried deep in snow, is what awaits snowshoers here. The length of the trail and the steepness with which it climbs are secondary considerations, however, for snowshoers will find an inordinate amount of natural beauty and winter wilderness on this trail. The beautiful little lake basin is situated in such a way that snowshoers who pause here for lunch may enjoy unmatched views of the whole of the Alpine Lakes Wilderness Area—from Mount Daniel to Mount Stuart—as well as the Glacier Peak Wilderness Area to the north, the Chelan-Sawtooth Wilderness to the east, and the beautiful Skykomish Valley to the west.

To get there, from Everett drive east on US 2 to the summit of Stevens Pass. Park in the ski area parking lots on the north side of the highway.

From the parking area, climb north along a groomed road leading past a number of small skier cabins on the edge of the forest above the highway. The groomed snow-cat track angles north away from the highway and ends abruptly near a power shack about a quarter mile up the slope. Dig your snowshoe cleats into the hillside, and continue straight up the hill. Stay near the trees on the west side of the open slope to minimize avalanche danger and collisions with telemark skiers whooshing down the slope. After nearly a mile of climbing, at the 5,000-foot elevation, the slope tapers off a bit and the climbing becomes easier. Pause here to catch your breath and soak in the views.

Turn and look south. At what seems just an arm's length away, the Stevens Pass Ski Area sprawls out across the slopes on the opposite side of the highway. Above and beyond those groomed runs (long, white scars on the dark green forest) stand the summits of the Alpine Lakes peaks. Mount

Lookout tower and weather station near Skyline Lake

Stuart, like a massive granite wall, looms in the southeast. Mount Daniel and Mount Hinman, the glaciated peaks in the center of the wilderness, rise like twin towers to the southwest. Nearer in, Thunder Mountain rises on the Cascade Crest just south of the ski area, and Bulls Tooth sits on the southern horizon.

After a well-deserved rest, continue climbing the now moderate slope, and in just a half mile, trudge through a young stand of fir to come upon the shores of Skyline Lake. At 5,000-feet elevation, this lake is generally high enough that the ice cap on it freezes solid enough to support skiers and snowshoers; indeed, the broad flat surface of the lake is almost always

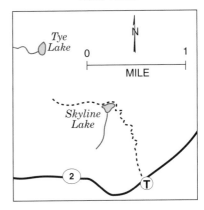

criss-crossed with ski and snowshoe tracks. Unless you have a desperate need to cross a frozen lake, however, it's always a good idea to skirt the lake's shore rather than risk the ice. The combination of generally mild winters and the volcanic nature of the Cascade Range makes all lake ice suspect. Even if temperatures are cold enough, long enough, to freeze a lake solid, the geothermal activity below the mountains creates a lot of warm and hot springs, some of which can spout out of the ground in the middle of a lake, keeping it warmer than you might expect. In effect, these unseen warm springs sometimes melt the surface ice from the underneath.

A long, relaxed lunch along the shores of the lake allows ample time to marvel at views to the south as well as the now-revealed vistas to the north, which include views of Glacier Peak and Lichtenburg Mountain. To extend the outing, amble west along the crest of Skyline Ridge for up to 2 miles more before returning to your car.

--39--

Lake Valhalla

Rating:	More difficult
Round trip:	7.5 miles
Hiking time:	5.5 hours
Elevation gain:	1,700 feet
High point:	4,800 feet
Best season:	December through early March
Maps:	Green Trails: Benchmark Mountain No. 144
Who to contact:	Wenatchee National Forest, Lake Wenatchee Ranger District

According to Norse mythology, Valhalla is the beautiful home of heroes slain in battle. Fortunately for snowshoers, this Valhalla is no myth, and visiting it doesn't require mortal combat. Lake Valhalla is a wondrously beautiful basin nestled alongside the Pacific Crest Trail just north of Stevens

Pass. Tucked between Mount McCausland and Lichtenburg Mountain, the lake appears remote and isolated. The snowshoe hike to the lake belies that wildness, though, because the trail is generally easy enough for novices and family groups.

Although summer hikers can access Lake Valhalla by way of the Pacific Crest Trail, snowshoers will find it easier, and safer, to make use of the narrow road leading up Smith Brook Valley to the east, and then traverse cross-country through the head of that valley to the lake basin. This path provides good footing, safety from avalanche danger, and stunning views along its route.

To get there, drive east on US 2 to the summit of Stevens Pass and continue another 6 miles east to the Mill Creek exit. Make a U-turn at Mill Creek to get into the westbound lanes of the divided highway, and drive west 1.2 miles to a narrow parking strip on the right (north) side of the highway. This is the nearest parking area to the Smith Brook Trailhead, which is another tenth of a mile to the west. With snowshoes in hand, follow the shoulder of the highway west to the start of Forest Service Road No. 6700 (Smith Brook Road). The plows will have left a high, vertical wall of snow between the road surface and the top of the untracked snow, so a climb is generally required. In heavy snow years, this embankment has been known to be as much as 18 feet high, but generally it is less than 10 feet. An ice ax can be handy here, not only for added traction in climbing but to chop out steps. If you don't want to chop your own, bear in mind that by mid-morning Saturday, on most winter weekends, someone will have dug a rough staircase into the bank.

The trail follows the narrow Smith Brook Road through a thin stand of forest along a near-level bench for the first quarter mile before beginning

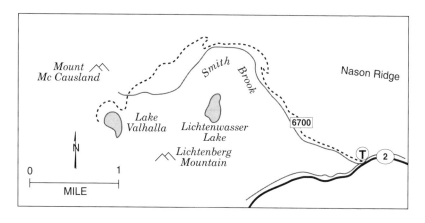

Forested hillside near Lake Valhalla

a gentle climb up the creek valley. The lower section of the valley has been logged, so the second-growth forest is dotted with clearcut sections for the first 1.5 miles of the hike. Look for birds and small animals where the forests and meadows meet: generally, camp-robber jays (a.k.a. whiskey jacks) flit through the area, and snowshoe hares leave tracks by the edges of the meadows.

At nearly 2 miles, the road switches back twice to gain elevation above the creek bed. Here, in the midst of a sloping clearcut meadow, some nice views open up west toward Mount McCausland and north to Union and Jove Peaks. The trail then follows the creek as it banks toward the west. Just over 2.5 miles up, at 4,000-feet elevation, the road again loops through a switchback turn.

This is the end of the road, but not the trail. Leave the road at the apex of that switchback, and traverse the open hillside above Smith Brook. Climb slightly while snowshoeing across the valley wall to get near the 4,600-foot level in the next mile. There, at 3.5 miles from the trailhead, catch the snow-obscured Pacific Crest Trail, cross the head of the Smith Brook Valley, and hike another quarter mile southwest to the Lake Valhalla Basin at 4,800 feet. Enjoy a rest at the lake while soaking in the views of Lichtenburg Mountain, Nason Ridge, Union and Jove Peaks, Mount McCausland, Valhalla Mountain, and Skyline Ridge to the south.

--40--

Surprise Lake

Rating: Backcountry
Round trip: 8 miles
Hiking time: 6 hours
Elevation gain: 2,300 feet
High point: 4,500 feet
Best season: December through early April
Maps: Green Trails: Stevens Pass No. 176
Who to contact: Mount Baker–Snoqualmie National Forest, Skykomish Ranger District

This trail limbs a narrow side valley above the Skykomish River, offering pretty views, sparkling waterfalls, and deep forest environments to explore and experience. The trail is popular with snowshoers, but don't expect to encounter many skiers here. The trail is far too narrow and the forest is way too close for most skiers' comfort.

All but the first half-mile of trail is within the Alpine Lakes Wilderness, so the forest is ancient, undisturbed old growth. That provides healthy habitat for an array of wildlife, and even in winter, a lot of scurrying and flittering occurs along the trail. Snowshoers can look for, and frequently see, animals such as martens, hares, and deer. They can also find tracks of cougars, bobcats, coyotes, and foxes, though these animals seldom allow themselves to be seen by humans. Birds in the area include the always-present whiskey jacks, ptarmigans, owls, ravens, falcons, and woodpeckers.

Descending a slope near Surprise Lake

Delicate waterfalls and deep blue pools are found along the plunging creek, and views of the rocky summits of Spark Plug and Thunder Mountains are spectacular along the upper end of the trail.

To get there, from Everett drive east on US 2 to the town of Skykomish and continue east another 10 miles. Turn right (south) into the small community of Scenic just before the railroad underpass on the highway. Cross the river, and turn right again onto a small spur road signed as the Surprise Creek/Surprise Lake Trailhead.

The snowshoe hike begins with a short walk up an old, narrow dirt road. Cross Surprise Creek about a half mile up, pass under the powerlines, and start up the Surprise Creek Valley proper. Just above the powerlines, the road gives way to a narrow hiking trail, at 2,200 feet, and begins to climb steadily. For a half mile, the trail stays well above the creek, but it then tapers down the valley wall and, at 1 mile, comes abreast of the creek and stays there most of the way to the lake. Several small side creeks are crossed, and near the 1.8-mile mark, the trail crosses to the west side of Surprise Creek.

Several small, unnamed waterfalls and miniature sets of rapids accent the little stream. These features are beautiful any time of year, but when the stream banks are cloaked in snow and the river rocks rimmed with ice, the tumbling waters are like sparkling jewels, glinting in the cold, winter sunshine.

At 3 miles, the trail leaves the creek side to climb west through a series of steep, tight switchbacks before banking south a bit and rolling the final quarter mile on fairly gentle slopes to the lakeshore. From the banks of the big lake, enjoy views of 6,311-foot Spark Plug Mountain to the west, Thunder Mountain (6,556 feet) to the south, and the deep Skykomish River Valley due north.

--*41*--

Lanham Lake

Rating:	More difficult
Round trip:	3.2 miles
Hiking time:	3 hours
Elevation gain:	1,100 feet
High point:	4,100 feet
Best season:	December through early March
Maps:	Green Trails: Benchmark Mountain No. 144
Who to contact:	Wenatchee National Forest, Lake Wenatchee Ranger District

This narrow forest trail climbs gently alongside a gurgling ice-rimmed creek and leads to a picturesque alpine lake. The trail is often attempted by cross-country skiers, but the narrow path and thick forest often send them packing before they complete the first mile, so a high degree of quiet solitude can be found at this lake despite the shortness of the access trail. The lake is ringed with snow-laden trees, but some nice views of the jagged

One of the snowy scenes that make snowshoeing so enjoyable

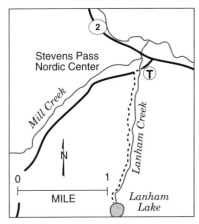

top of Jim Hill Mountain appear to the south. The lake is also an ideal destination for novice winter campers—not too far to snowshoe but far enough to get into a true wilderness setting. The thick old growth around the lake provides plenty of shelter for a snug winter camp.

To get there, drive east on US 2 to the summit of Stevens Pass and continue another 6 miles east to the Mill Creek exit. Turn right onto Mill Creek Road, and drive a few hundred feet to park in the Mill Creek Sno-Park (the lower lot). The lot nearest the buildings is provided for the commercial nordic ski facilities run by the Stevens Pass Ski Area. To avoid conflicts, avoid snowshoeing on the groomed trails wherever possible.

The Lanham Lake Trail starts about 10 yards up Mill Creek Road—one of the ski area's groomed trails—so snowshoe along the uphill edge of this groomed track to avoid incurring the wrath of skiers on your way to the trailhead. Bear left into the trees at the well-marked start of the Lanham Lake Trail.

This narrow hikers' trail follows the west bank of Lanham Creek as it climbs the gentle valley to its headwaters in the lake. About a quarter mile up, the trail crosses a clearing, passes under high tension powerlines—these carry the juice that keeps Puget Sounders out of the dark—and crosses a groomed ski trail (part of the commercial operation).

Try to ignore the buzzing electrical lines and the unnaturally flat track left by the groomer. The trail leaves both behind quickly as it continues the steady climb up the creek valley. About a mile up the trail, the valley narrows considerably. The trail is now close to the creek, and footing is sometimes slick where the trail enters a brief, steep pitch for a couple hundred yards.

The last half mile is only moderately steep as the valley widens again and finally opens into a deep bowl cradling the lake. If you are the adventurous type, trek up the slope on the far (south) side of the lake to explore the flanks of Jim Hill Mountain, but if avalanche danger is moderate or higher, skip this added adventure and stick to the lake basin for any extra exploration.

--42--

Wenatchee Ridge

Rating:	Easiest to more difficult
Round trip:	10 miles
Hiking time:	7 hours
Elevation gain:	2,000 feet
High point:	4,050 feet
Best season:	January through late February
Maps:	Green Trails: Wenatchee Lake No. 145
Who to contact:	Wenatchee National Forest, Lake Wenatchee Ranger District

This trail combines the serene beauty of the Little Wenatchee River Valley with the thrilling vistas found on the high benches of Wenatchee Ridge. Trek the entire route to climb to those panoramic views of peaks and ridges of the eastern Cascades, or stick to the lower half of the route and enjoy a quiet day in a picturesque mountain valley.

Kids will love the flat, snowy track along the Little Wenatchee River,

Ice formation on a rocky outcropping near the crest of Wenatchee Ridge

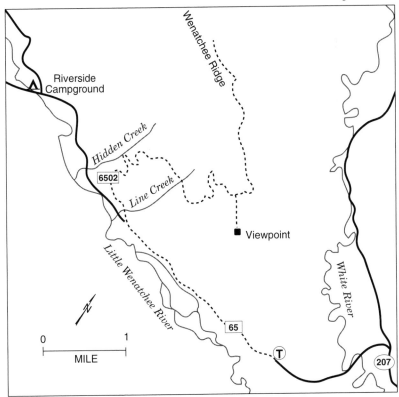

and families can make a day of it by hiking along the valley bottom, reveling in the musical sounds of the river splashing over the icy rocks of its bed. Nice views up to the jagged crest of Wenatchee Ridge to the north and the high, snowy crowns of Mount Mastiff and Mount Howard to the south round out this part of the trail.

Adventurers will love the moderate climb up the snout of Wenatchee Ridge, with strikingly beautiful views across the valley toward those two great peaks, Mastiff and Howard, which anchor the northern end of Nason Ridge.

To get there, from Leavenworth drive north on US 2 to Coles Corner and turn right (north) onto Highway 207. Continue north on Highway 207 for 11 miles, passing Lake Wenatchee, and turn left (west) onto the Little Wenatchee River Road (Forest Service Road No. 65). Drive 1.5 miles to a Sno-Park area at the end of the plowed road.

Hike Road No. 65 as it heads upstream alongside Little Wenatchee River. Actually, the road is several hundred feet from the river, with some broad meadows and thin groves of alder and pine between, but a mile up the valley, the road and river come together to provide some water-side entertainment. Look for the quick movements of water ouzels—small birds dipping in and out of the frigid waters—and small flotillas of ducks in the pools of the stream.

At 2 miles, a side road (Forest Service Road No. 6502) angles off to the right. This is the route up the ridge. Snowshoe up it as it traverses for a half mile before climbing more steeply through a wide series of switchbacks. Road No. 6502 passes three side roads in its first mile—stay left at the first main intersection and right at the next two. At mile 3, the track begins a long curving traverse east around the snout of the ridge. There are some nice views through openings in the forest cover. Looking south over the Little Wenatchee Valley, Nason Ridge—anchored on the west by Mount Mastiff and on the east by Round Mountain—is seen.

At mile 4, the route turns sharply to the left to climb around a small knob at 3,300 feet. The road continues to climb gradually for the last 1.5 miles, rolling around to the north side of the ridge before ending at 4,000 feet before the jagged crest of the ridge.

--43--

Chiwaukum Creek

Rating:	More difficult
Round trip:	10.4 miles
Hiking time:	6 hours to 2 days
Elevation gain:	1,200 feet
High point:	3,200 feet
Best season:	December through early March
Maps:	Green Trails: Chiwaukum Mountains No. 177
Who to contact:	Wenatchee National Forest, Leavenworth Ranger District

This narrow wilderness trail follows the Chiwaukum Creek upstream to a junction with several other trails, providing opportunities for unbounded rambling in the winter wonderlands of the Alpine Lakes Wilderness. Most snowshoers, though, will find plenty of beautiful country, awesome views, and outstanding snowshoeing along the first 5 miles of the trail. The trail pierces beautiful pine and fir forests, nicely blanketed in pristine white snow.

Snow pillows on the rocks in a small tributary creek in the Chiwaukum Valley

Along the way, snowshoers can gawk in wonder at the towering ramparts of Big Jim and Snowgrass Mountains. They can enjoy the musical stylings of Chiwaukum Creek as it bounds over ice-crusted boulders and snow-laden logs. And, unfortunately, they can skip the whole thing if the avalanche danger is moderate or higher. The first mile of trail is at the base of a steep, slide-prone slope and should only be crossed when the risk of avalanche is low or nonexistent. But if the conditions are right, this trail is not to be missed.

To get there, from Leavenworth drive north on US 2 about 9 miles to Tumwater Campground. Continue north another mile and turn left onto Chiwaukum Creek Road (Forest Service Road No. 7908). Drive 2 miles to the end of the road, at 2,200 feet, or to the snow line if it is lower than that. The trailhead is at the road end.

Chiwaukum Creek cuts through a narrow valley along its lower reaches. Because the last mile of the road and the first mile of trail are at the base of steep, avalanche-prone slopes, this is a trail for stable snow days only. But on those days, this trail is marvelous. It is nearly flat, gaining just 1,200 feet in more than 5 miles, and it pierces some of the most beautiful old forests of pine and fir in the region. The ponderosa pine is particularly pretty in this setting, with its bright-orange bark scales offsetting the brilliant white of the snow and the sparkling blue of the creek.

The trail rolls upstream, curving gently to the west and opening up views of McCue Ridge towering above the upper Chiwaukum Creek Valley and Big Jim Mountain to the south. Numerous wide areas in the sheltering forests offer excellent sites in which to pitch a camp, and the possibilities of making an extended snowshoeing adventure out of this trip are endless. At 5.2 miles the trail splits. This is where most of you will turn back, but if you are a hearty winter fanatic, consider pushing on into the deeper regions of the Alpine Lakes Wilderness. Do this only if you are adequately prepared for *extended* winter exposure.

At the trail fork, the path on the right climbs steeply to Chiwaukum Lake and Larch Lake Basins. This trail crosses several avalanche slopes and is best left for summer explorations. The left trail, though, follows the South Fork of Chiwaukum River for 3 miles, passing several other trails along the way. Good campsites are found at Timothy Meadows, about 2 miles upstream from the original trail split.

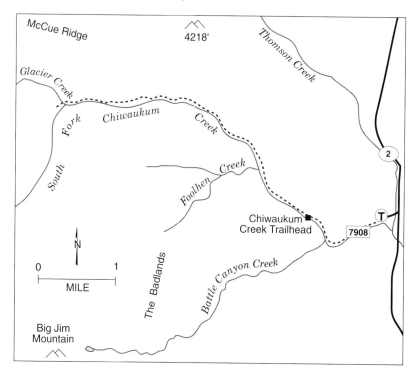

--44--

Eight-mile Creek

Rating:	Backcountry
Round trip:	12.4 miles
Hiking time:	1 to 2 days
Elevation gain:	2,600 feet
High point:	4,600 feet
Best season:	December through early March
Maps:	Green Trails: Chiwaukum Mountains No. 177
Who to contact:	Wenatchee National Forest, Leavenworth Ranger District

One of the most heavily visited trails in summer, the Eight-mile Trail is virtually ignored by winter recreationists. Cross-country skiers find the narrow trail and occasionally steep pitches difficult to navigate while wearing their long boards, but today's snowshoes are tailor-made for tromping in and around tightly spaced trees and up steep slopes.

On the road leading toward the backcountry trail up Eight-mile Creek

In addition to quiet solitude, this trail offers unmatched wilderness beauty. High alpine lakes appear in table-flat meadows covered by blankets of billowing white fluff. Crystalline creeks rush through icy channels alongside the trail. Above it all towers the monarch of the central Cascades—Mount Stuart. Joining that great bulk on the horizon are Cannon, Eight-mile, and Cashmere Mountains. This trail can be more tiring than one might think, but don't fret if forced to turn back before reaching the upper end of the trail. There is plenty to see and enjoy on the lower half of this route to make even an abbreviated snowshoe trek here worthwhile.

Bear in mind that this trail is at the bottom of a narrow valley in steep mountain country, so avalanche hazards are extreme. Knowledge of how to recognize and avoid avalanche dangers is essential for visitors on this trail.

To get there, from Leavenworth drive north on US 2 and, at the northern edge of town, turn left (west) onto Icicle Creek Road. Continue west 8.5 miles to Bridge Creek Campground. Turn left onto Forest Service Road No. 7601, and park near the bridge over Icicle Creek. In heavy snow years, it may be necessary to park farther down the valley and snowshoe a few miles up Icicle Creek Road to Bridge Creek Campground (2,000 feet). In light snow years, it is sometimes possible to drive another mile or so up Road No. 7601 before being stopped at the snow line. Mileage figures for the hike are measured from Bridge Creek Campground.

The snowshoeing begins on the wide, moderately pitched Road No. 7601. This road contours along the hillside above Mountaineer Creek, gaining just 1,300 feet in the 3 miles to the junction with Eight-mile Creek. The lower valley is wide and scenic, providing plenty of pretty views south to Cannon Mountain and east to Icicle Ridge. At 3 miles, the road crosses Eight-mile Creek. Instead of crossing the creek with the road, turn right and start up the narrow Eight-mile Creek Trail which weaves through the tight forest of pine and fir on the lower flanks of Cashmere Mountain.

The trail climbs gently for nearly a mile until, at 4 miles out, the route steepens as the valley narrows. At times, the trail is obscured completely, and routefinding skills are tested. But getting lost isn't much of a threat because the trail parallels the creek, so routefinding is merely an exercise in finding the most efficient path up the steep slopes. Fortunately, the steepest pitch is only a few hundred feet long. Then the trail returns to its moderate pitch. In fact, there is a mere 1,100-foot gain from the point where the trail leaves the road to Little Eight-mile Lake, encountered at 5.7 miles. Some potential campsites are found around this little pond, but much better sites can be found a half mile farther up the valley—and another 200 feet higher in elevation—at Eight-mile Lake.

This sprawling plain of ice and snow is in the shadow of Eight-mile Mountain, which looms to the north, and you will find that a camp here is blessed with magnificent sunrises. Watching the morning sky brighten and seeing the icy face of Eight-mile Mountain glow with dawn's orange light is an experience of a lifetime.

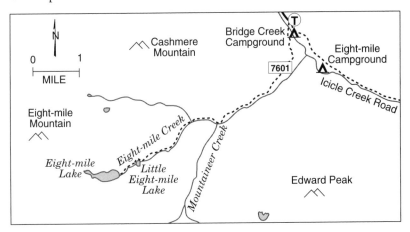

--45--

Talapus Lake

Rating: Most difficult
Round trip: 10.5 miles
Hiking time: 7 hours
Elevation gain: 1,600 feet
High point: 3,280 feet
Best season: January through early March
Maps: Green Trails: Bandera No. 206
Who to contact: Mount Baker–Snoqualmie National Forest, North Bend Ranger District

Overcrowded in summer months, this trail is too often overlooked in the winter. Sure, the route requires a modest hike up a snowy road before getting to the trailhead, but that's the perfect way for snowshoers to warm up and swing into stride. The trail ascends through open fir and hemlock forests, dips low and rolls alongside a pretty mountain stream a time or two, and finally deposits dedicated snowshoers on the shores of a wide, pretty alpine

Taking a break along the trail to Talapus Lake

lake nestled below a steep, avalanche-ravaged ridge. The views from the lake basin include looks up at Bandera Mountain, Pratt Mountain, and east to Granite Mountain.

The trail is easy to find, although it can be a bit difficult to follow if the snow is crusty and slick. Be sure to have good cleats on both heel and toe to ensure a solid "bite" on the crusty snow that is often the curse of this trail.

To get there, from North Bend drive east on Interstate 90 for 15 miles to Exit 45. After exiting the Interstate, turn left, cross under the freeway, and follow Forest Service Road No. 9031 west 1 mile to its junction with Forest Service Road No. 9030 on the right. Park here, or if the road isn't plowed, park at the end of the plowed area, well clear of the freeway exits, and snowshoe the mile to Road No. 9030.

Start up Road No. 9030, signed as the access to Talapus Lake Trailhead, as it rolls up through a series of small switchbacks. The road offers good views up-slope toward the summit of Bandera Mountain thanks to several open clearcut areas that flank the road. The 2.5 miles of the road hike goes fast. At the end of the road, in the wide parking area of the Talapus Lake Trailhead, enjoy stunning views of Granite Mountain before starting up the narrow trail.

Usually you will have the trail to yourself from this point on. Skiers often kick their way up the road as far as the trailhead, but few of those folks care to struggle with their long skis on the winding, forest trail. With snowshoes, you will have no problems with the twisting, turning trail as it rolls around trees and rocks. At 3.5 miles, after a mile of snowshoeing on the narrow trail, the path dips into a valley to follow close alongside Talapus Creek the last three-quarters of a mile to the lake.

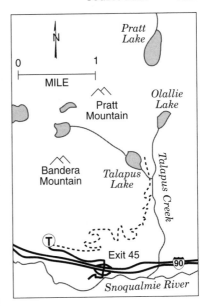

The lake basin is the most likely place to find snowslides, so as you approach the lake, be aware of avalanche potentials. If the avalanche hazard was reported as moderate or higher for this part of the Cascades, it's best to skip the trail component of this outing. The roadway makes a nice, gentle outing on snowshoes, without the danger of being swept away.

--46--

Source Lake

Rating:	More difficult
Round trip:	Up to 10 miles
Hiking time:	7 hours
Elevation gain:	2,300 feet
High point:	5,300 feet
Best season:	January through early March
Maps:	Green Trails: Snoqualmie Pass No. 207
Who to contact:	Mount Baker–Snoqualmie National Forest, North Bend Ranger District

The Snow Lake Trail is possibly the most heavily used wilderness trail in the state, so snowshoers who hike here may be surprised to find so few fellow snowshoers on the route with them. Sure, when the snow is unstable, avalanche dangers are scary. But when the conditions are stable and the avalanche danger is listed as moderate or lower, the trail to Source Lake

A slab of snow calving off at the base of a steep avalanche slope above Source Lake

(and on up to Snow Lake) makes a wonderful outing for snowshoers.

On the moderate, short hike to Source Lake, snowshoers can bask in glorious views of Denny Mountain, The Tooth, Bryant Peak, Chair Peak, and Snoqualmie Mountain. Those with sharp eyes can sometimes spot radical extreme-skiers sneaking away from the Alpental Ski Area to launch themselves down the near-vertical snow-laden slopes of these peaks. Those who would rather watch a more natural variety of wildlife can scan the skies to spot red-tailed hawks, golden eagles, ravens, and falcons. Martens, hares, weasels, and squirrels burrow through and scamper over the snow around the trail.

To get there, from Seattle drive east on Interstate 90 to exit 52 (Snoqualmie Pass, West Summit) and turn north, crossing under the freeway. Continue north to the end of the road at the Alpental Ski Area parking lot.

Start by either finding the Snow Lake Trailhead on the east side of the lower parking lot and following it as it climbs up the slope before looping northwest or go the easier route and, from the upper end of the parking area, snowshoe cross-country up the slope at the base of Snoqualmie Mountain to catch the trail as it passes the ski area.

The trail climbs at a gentle pitch up the Snoqualmie River Valley, passing through alder thickets, old stands of forest, and open meadows, for 1.5 miles—gaining more than 700 feet along the way—before curving sharply to the left. If the snow's not too deep, look for a trail sign indicating the Snow Lake Trail climbing steeply to the right. That summer route is a bit too hairy for snowshoes, so head for Source Lake instead by hiking nearly due west on a level traverse for a half mile. The lake is a small, circular tarn at the base of a steep wall below Chair Peak. This is the headwaters of the South Fork Snoqualmie River, although in winter, with its thick ice cap, it looks more like a flat bench than a deep lake. Enjoy a rest and picnic here while soaking in the views of the surrounding panorama. Denny Peak lies to the south, flanked by The Tooth, Bryant Peak, and Chair Peak to the west. To the north, a high ridge links Chair Peak to Snoqualmie Peak on the

northeast, which is in turn flanked by Lundin Peak, Red Mountain, and finally Guye Peak to the southeast.

If the snow is very stable and you are an adventurous sort, head for the top of the ridge separating Source Lake from Snow Lake, angling north up the open face of the ridge toward a tuft of trees at the ridge crest. The climb is steep, strenuous, and recommended only for experienced snowshoe mountaineers.

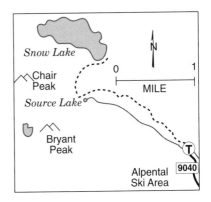

--*47*--

Commonwealth Basin

Rating:	Backcountry
Round trip:	Up to 10 miles
Hiking time:	7 hours
Elevation gain:	2,300 feet
High point:	5,300 feet
Best season:	January through early March
Maps:	Green Trails: Snoqualmie Pass No. 207
Who to contact:	Mount Baker–Snoqualmie National Forest, North Bend Ranger District

See Page 152 for map.

The section of the Pacific Crest Trail north of Snoqualmie Pass is overrun with hikers every summer weekend, but put a few feet of snow on the trail, and the crowds ignore it. That's great news for snowshoers because the trail is easy to get to and enjoyable for snowshoeing. The route to Commonwealth Basin follows the Pacific Crest Trail for more than 2 miles through shadowy old-growth forest—with an occasional break in the trees for views of the surrounding peaks—before setting off on a smaller path into the wide, rocky basin at the base of Red Mountain.

Snowshoer trudging over drifted snow in the upper Commonwealth Basin

Commonwealth Basin affords excellent views of the iron-rich flanks of Red Mountain, although snowshoers will be at a loss to explore the source for the mountain's name since it is covered in a deep quilt of white snow all winter. There are also excellent views up to Kendall Peak and Snoqualmie Mountain from the basin, while the trail leading into the area is surrounded by gorgeous forests of cedar, hemlock, and fir.

To get there, from Seattle drive east on Interstate 90 to exit 52 (Snoqualmie Pass, West Summit) and turn north, crossing under the freeway. Continue north to the first wide, plowed pullout along the road, usually no more than a quarter mile beyond the freeway. Park in the first available space, making sure your vehicle is well clear of the roadway. If parking is not available on the lower road, park on the south side of the freeway and walk through the underpass to reach the trailhead.

Just north of the freeway underpass, a small snow-covered road climbs off to the right. Snowshoe up this road into a wide summer parking area at the Pacific Crest Trailhead. The trail leads off from the east end of the parking lot, rolling up through thick forest on a long traverse to the east before looping through a switchback corner near 0.7 mile and climbing northwest. After looping through a couple more short switchbacks, the trail rolls north to a junction at 2.5 miles (4,000 feet).

An alternate route, when snow is very deep, is to snowshoe up the narrow valley directly above the PCT parking area. Stay left and climb through the trees, keeping the small creek basin on your left until reaching the broad mouth of Commonwealth Basin.

The route to this point is easy to follow because the trail corridor is wide and obvious in the heavy forest. The trail stays under the forest canopy nearly all of the first 2.5 miles, although it does cross the base of a large avalanche slope and then recross the slope higher up after climbing through a switchback. Cross this slope with care, and if the avalanche danger is higher than moderate, avoid the area. The point where the trail crosses the slope is on the run-out section of the chute rather than the trigger area, so it is unlikely that you will trigger a slide here, but caution is still required.

At the trail junction, stay left—the Pacific Crest Trail climbs steadily to the right—and follow the Commonwealth Creek Valley up into the basin. The trail is a long, straight ascent up the valley, climbing gradually as it enters the basin. The forest thins, and finally falls away at 4 miles, leaving you on open slopes at the base of Red Mountain. Potential for avalanches exists here beyond timber line, so care and common sense must be used in heavy doses. If the snow is stable and safe, it's possible to scramble up to the 5,300-foot level (about 5 miles from the trailhead) at a low saddle on the ridge between Red Mountain and Lundin Peak. The last half mile of climbing is steep and should be attempted only by those with experience in snowshoe mountaineering.

--48--

Kendall Peak Lakes

Rating:	Most difficult
Round trip:	9 miles
Hiking time:	7 hours
Elevation gain:	1,700 feet
High point:	4,400 feet
Best season:	January through early March
Maps:	Green Trails: Snoqualmie Pass No. 207
Who to contact:	Mount Baker–Snoqualmie National Forest, North Bend Ranger District
	See page 152 for map.

The roar of the highway noise is unmistakable when starting up this track, but soon the beauty of the winter wilderness surrounding the trail makes everything else fade into the background. The dark green firs and hemlocks lining the ridge, the open, quilted meadows of snow, and the wide avenue of the trail make this a perfect destination for snowshoers.

The trail leads to a pair of small alpine ponds nestled in a deep cirque on the flank of towering Kendall Peak (5,675 feet). The mountain dominates the skyline from the lakes basin, as well as along the last mile of the trail leading into the basin. But Kendall isn't the only peak on the horizon. To the east is Alta Mountain and the long line of Rampart Ridge. To the south is Mount Catherine with its lower flanks lined with the wide white slashes of alpine ski runs. Below the lakes, the broad meadows along the bottom of Gold Creek Valley glimmer a brilliant white in the afternoon sun.

Although the trail ascends nearly 2,000 feet, the climbing is gradual and the trail is easy to follow. Because of that, first-time 'shoers and young kids will enjoy this outing as much as experienced snowshoe enthusiasts.

Of course, all of those features coupled with the trail's close proximity to the Seattle metropolitan area means a lot of snowshoers and skiers on any winter weekend. Strap on the snowshoes midweek, though, and the trail will be virtually deserted.

Mother and child on lower section of Kendall Peak Lakes route

To get there, from Seattle drive east on Interstate 90 over Snoqualmie Pass to Exit 54, found 2 miles east of the pass's summit. Exit I-90, turn left, and cross under the freeway to reach the Gold Creek Sno-Park just a few hundred feet north of the highway interchange.

Snowshoe up the Gold Creek Valley, staying close to the left (west) side of the valley, and in a few hundred yards, find an old logging road climbing left into the trees on the valley wall. This road is steep for a quarter mile, and then the ascent moderates considerably. The road enters an old clearcut just past the half-mile mark and twists and turns its way up the slope. You can either stay with the moderate pitch of the road or take a steeper, more direct, northerly approach straight up the slope, cutting off the switchback corners. Pause often to rest. Use the excuse of stopping to admire the increasingly pretty views south over the Gold Creek Basin, Hyak Ski Area, and Mount Catherine if you are the competitive sort who doesn't like to admit to fatigue!

At 1.7 miles, the trail hooks through a sharp hairpin turn to the right. A wide spur road heads off to the left, leading to a nice overlook of the lower Coal Creek Basin and the ski areas of Snoqualmie Summit and Ski Acres. Stay right if you are bound for the lakes. The road traverses east toward the snout of a narrow ridge and, at that leading edge of the ridge, turns north and climbs steeply through forest and meadow. The track stays on the west side of the ridge crest, banking right at 2.6 miles, and at 3.5 miles, hooking sharply south in a switchback turn.

Stay north, snowshoeing off the road at the apex of the hairpin corner, to find a narrow path just below the ridge crest leading to Kendall Lakes. The trail nears Coal Creek at 4.2 miles and follows it the remainder of the way to the lakes' basin, rolling over two small knolls before reaching the lower of the twin Kendall Lakes. Avoid the upper lake because the tight, avalanche-prone walls of the cirque are not a safe way to approach it.

--49--

Lower Gold Creek Basin

Rating:	Easiest to more difficult
Round trip:	7 miles
Hiking time:	5 hours
Elevation gain:	400 feet
High point:	3,000 feet
Best season:	December through February
Maps:	Green Trails: Snoqualmie Pass No. 207
Who to contact:	Mount Baker–Snoqualmie National Forest, North Bend Ranger District

See page 152 for map.

Hiking through a wide, level valley in the shadow of looming Kendall Peak to the north and Rampart Ridge to the east would be an ideal outing, if only so many people didn't know about it. Fortunately, a few miles up the trail, the crowds thin—or at least spread out—and snowshoers can get on with the business of learning to travel in a beautiful wilderness valley. That's right, just a few miles after leaving the buzzing I-90 corridor, the Alpine Lakes Wilderness unfolds. By mid-December, the snow is usually deep enough for the outing to be enjoyable, making this a great destination for families who gave each other snowshoes for Christmas.

To get there, from Seattle drive east on Interstate 90 over Snoqualmie Pass to Exit 54, found 2 miles east of the pass's summit. Exit I-90, turn left, cross under the freeway, and just a few hundred feet north of the highway interchange, turn right onto a narrow paved road and drive east parallel to the freeway for 1 mile. Cars generally line both sides of this road as the shoulder is the primary parking area for the long Gold Creek Sno-Park. Park at the end of the plowed road, near the small bridge over the stream connecting Mardee Lake to Lake Keechelus.

Start the hike by heading north along a narrow access road (Forest Service Road No. 144) on the eastern side of Mardee Lake. The road stays tight to the eastern wall of the valley, but if the snow is deep enough to bury all the ground cover, drop off the road in a few hundred yards—just past Mardee Lake—and snowshoe up the open meadow and through the thin stands of forest. As you hike up the valley, the view of Kendall Peak gets better and better, while on your right, Rampart Ridge rolls majestically along. As the valley tapers in, the meadows give way to wide stands of trees and small forest clearings. The walls close in tighter and tighter on the valley floor, and the views become more dramatic. At about 3.5 miles in, stop and enjoy the scenery and the feeling of power that this winter wilderness emits.

At the northern end of Rampart Ridge is the bulky summit of Alta Mountain; directly opposite is the vertical face of Kendall Peak. The steep walls of these mountains seem to rise from the ground at your feet. Continue to press on up the valley, but only if you know how to evaluate avalanche dangers. Even on the valley floor, hikers are susceptible to avalanches. The mammoth slides can come barreling off the valley walls with enough momentum that they sweep well out onto the basin's floor.

If you are seeking more adventure, continue on up the middle of the valley floor for another 2.5 miles, crossing in front of the mouth of Silver Creek Valley on the north side of Kendall Peak, before reaching a small

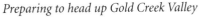

Preparing to head up Gold Creek Valley

draw leading off to the left. This is the outlet stream from Alaska Lake. Leave Gold Creek, and begin your ascent of the valley wall here, heading north-northwest. The lake is just 1 mile up the slope, but the elevation gain in that mile is more than 1,000 feet, so take your time.

Alaska Lake fills a small basin directly below Alaska Mountain and Ridge Lake, which both lie alongside the Pacific Crest Trail. Steep walls surround the lake, except at the outlet end, so plan your camp there to avoid potential avalanche chutes. Although the lake will most likely be frozen over, stay off the ice because it is usually thin and subject to cracking.

--50--
Mount Margaret

Rating:	Easiest to more difficult
Round trip:	9 miles
Hiking time:	6 hours
Elevation gain:	2,800 feet
High point:	3,600 feet
Best season:	Late December through late February
Maps:	Green Trails: Snoqualmie Pass No. 207
Who to contact:	Wenatchee National Forest, Cle Elum Ranger District
	See page 152 for map.

Views of the entire eastern half of the Snoqualmie Pass area, including the sprawling blue waters of Keechelus Lake and the snow-covered summits of Mount Catherine and Tinkham Peak to the south, can be had from the upper reaches of this route. The lower section, though, is unremarkable. The flat roadway, parallel to noisy I-90, is a great place for novice snowshoers to get a feel for hiking with the broad "foot boards," and it does serve as a good warm-up for the long climb ahead. The real treasures of the Mount Margaret trek are found beyond the second mile.

Because this area is close to the metropolitan centers, a lot of skiers and snowshoers share the trail. That, combined with the closeness of the busy freeway, means the chances of seeing wildlife are pretty slim. Still, where people play in the woods, camp-robber jays look for handouts. This valley is also patrolled by many red-tailed hawks and ravens, so watch the skies for raptors and corvids, and look for the tiny tracks of their prey (mice, hares, and grouse) in the meadows.

To get there, from Seattle drive east on Interstate 90 over Snoqualmie Pass to Exit 54, found 2 miles east of the pass's summit. Exit I-90, turn left, cross under the freeway, and just a few hundred feet north of the highway interchange, turn right onto a narrow paved road and drive east parallel to the freeway for 1 mile. Cars generally line both sides of this road as the shoulder is the primary parking area for the long Gold Creek Sno-Park. Park at the end of the plowed road, near the small bridge over the stream connecting Mardee Lake to Keechelus Lake.

The first 1.5 miles of the snowshoe hike follow the road southeast from the parking area, parallel to I-90. This leg of the journey is frequently used by cross-country skiers who are just learning their craft, and it makes a nice place to familiarize yourself with your snowshoes. The road curves around the base of Rampart Ridge, with just a few modest views west toward Mount Catherine and Roaring Ridge above the waters of Keechelus Lake.

After crossing Wolfe Creek, the road climbs gradually, switches back to recross the creek, and just a few hundred yards beyond the second crossing, switches back once more to start a long, traversing climb through intermittent forest and clearcuts to mile 2.5. Two more switchbacks are encountered in the next half mile, and at 3.2 miles, the road splits. The left fork continues to climb while the right stays at a level traverse before dropping toward the I-90 valley. Staying left, climb for another half mile to

View over the valley from below Mount Margaret

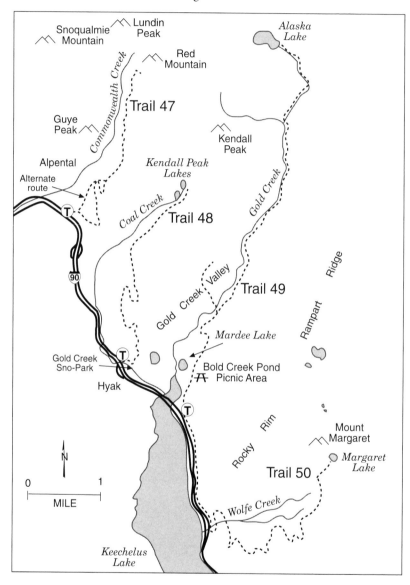

3,600 feet and a gate marking the Mount Margaret Trailhead.

The trail is wide for a hiking path—it's actually an old jeep road—so it is very easy to follow even when deep in snow. The path zig-zags steeply up the side of a ridge, through broad clearcut meadows. Save some travel time by angling east, still climbing steeply, to the eastern edge of a large meadow. Pause here to soak in the views of the Snoqualmie Pass area, Keechelus

Lake, and the sprawling clearcut-pocked mountains of the South Cascades. On clear days, Mount Rainier and sometimes even Mount Adams are visible to the south.

Continue uphill toward the ridge crest (now heading north), following the road through a small forested area, another meadow, and finally a solid, respectable stand of trees. The last half mile is along a true hiking trail in deep forest. It climbs, weaving around trees, along the crest of the ridge to a high promontory below the craggy summit of Mount Margaret. Below, on the eastern side of the ridge, is tiny Margaret Lake. Reaching its shores, though, requires a steep descent along an avalanche-prone slope, so stay on the ridge and enjoy the wonderful views.

--51--
Keechelus Ridge

Rating:	More difficult
Round trip:	6.4 miles
Hiking time:	5 hours
Elevation gain:	2,100 feet
High point:	4,900 feet
Best season:	Late January through late February
Maps:	Green Trails: Snoqualmie Pass No. 207
Who to contact:	Wenatchee National Forest, Cle Elum Ranger District

Snowshoers who like to climb will love this route. Although the trail is broad and easy to follow all the way to the ridge crest, ample opportunities exist for snowshoers who want to show off their climbing abilities by heading straight up the open slopes.

But this trail isn't all work. Plenty of rewards await the dedicated athletes who point their snowshoes toward the top of this ridge. Best of all, even those who cut their trips short of the top will find the journey pays off tremendously. Views from the route are incredible, and the higher snowshoers go, the better the panoramic scenery. The jumbled peaks of the South Cascades spread away to the southern horizon with Mount Rainier dominating the skyline.

To get there, from Seattle drive east on Interstate 90 over Snoqualmie Pass to Exit 62, signed Kachess Lake, about 10 miles east of the pass's summit. After exiting the interstate, turn left, cross over the freeway, and turn left onto the freeway on-ramp and drive westbound I-90 for 1.5 miles to

the Price Creek Westbound Sno-Park. (Although another Sno-Park is located on the other side of the freeway, there is no way to cross the interstate to reach it.)

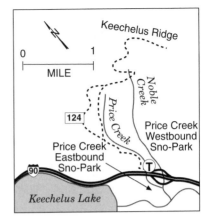

A small trail leads northwest from the Sno-Park for a quarter mile to Forest Service Road No. 4832. Turn left and hike west a couple hundred feet to leave the multi-use crowds behind. (Snowmobilers, skiers, skijorers [skiers pulled by one or more dogs], and even dogsledders use this trail.)

Climb to the right onto a small side road, Forest Service Road No. 124. This road climbs steeply up the flank of Keechelus Ridge alongside Price Creek for a half mile before angling west away from the creek in a long, looping route that isn't too steep but does cover several miles. You can choose to stick with the road, but a faster, more enjoyable route is to head cross-country up the slope, slicing across old clearcuts and thin stands of forest.

The best cross-country "trail" is found about 1.3 miles out from the Sno-Park. As the road rolls farther west away from Price Creek, snowshoe up the slope away from the track, staying right while the road goes left. Parallel Price Creek uphill, but stay on the bench above the stream rather than descending into the brambles alongside it. The slope rolls upward over several small benches and false summits, crossing clearcut, old and new. In light snow years, take care to avoid hooking a snowshoe on some of the brush protruding in the older, grown-over cuts. The climb covers about a mile of distance before crossing another heavily used road, Forest Service Road No. 4934, just below the ridge crest (4,300 feet). Emerge onto that road at about the same place as Road No. 124, which finally loops back from its long journey around the ridge flank.

Rather than joining Road No. 4934—a popular snowmobile route that creates a long loop when coupled with several other roads in the area— merely snowshoe across it, and head toward the ridge crest. This last half mile of climbing is also cross-country travel, although you can follow the road (Road No. 124) here too, if you are nervous about routefinding on the open ridge. The top is easily identifiable on the approach by tall radio-relay towers. At the top, put the towers behind you (thus keeping them out of sight) and enjoy the panoramic vistas of the eastern Cascades.

Icicles on evergreen bough

--52--

Amabilis Mountain

Rating: Most difficult
Round trip: 8 miles
Hiking time: 6 hours
Elevation gain: 2,100 feet
High point: 4,554 feet
Best season: Late January through late February
Maps: Green Trails: Snoqualmie Pass No. 207
Who to contact: Wenatchee National Forest, Cle Elum Ranger District

Sometimes it's nice to cut a switchback or two; to go where skiers and snowmobilers can't; to work up a sweat on a cold day while enjoying spectacular local scenery and distant views. This trail offers all that. A road loops, bobs, and weaves its way to the top of the mountain, but snowshoers don't need roads. There is enough open country on the side of the mountain that snowshoers can just point their shoes uphill and go, jumping onto the road when necessary to avoid particularly steep pitches or brambly clearcuts.

All that open country makes prime hunting habitat for raptors—red-tailed hawks and falcons—and ravens. Owls prowl the forest fringes, and bald eagles soar through between fishing trips up the Yakima River. Those birds are here for a reason, and that reason is rabbits, or more accurately, hares. Snowshoe hares, which bound through the meadows and burrow in the snow to eat the grasses underneath. Even if the white rabbits aren't seen, their tracks frequently are.

This route is steep and has a high danger of avalanche at times, so avoid the mountain when forecasters report avalanche dangers are moderate or higher.

To get there, from Seattle drive east on Interstate 90 over Snoqualmie Pass to Exit 63, signed Cabin Creek. Turn right after exiting the interstate, and enter the Cabin Creek Sno-Park on the right.

Before strapping on the snowshoes, walk north across the freeway overpass and find the start of Forest Service Road No. 4826 on the left. Snowshoe north on this wide, flat road. Note that the road is usually groomed, with tracks frequently set for skiers (twin, parallel grooves carved

Looking up the valley, Amabilis Mountain route

into the snow by a grooming machine), so steer your snowshoes well clear of the tracks. A quarter mile up the road, turn off onto Forest Service Road No. 4822 and start to climb toward the summit of Amabilis. This trail switches back and forth a few times before slanting off to the south on a long traverse of the middle section of the mountain.

Cross a small creek, and at about 2 miles, the trail forks. A hard hairpin turn to the left leads you on a long looping route to the mountaintop. Snowshoeing straight off on the right-hand road leads to an even longer loop to the same point at the summit (which, incidentally, is almost directly up-slope from this intersection).

Either road will get you to the top, but if you are looking to avoid the roads, start off along the left fork, and in a half mile, leave the road by climbing on a more direct route up the slope while still slanting slightly to the left. The views are now spectacular. Looking south and west, the Yakima River and Lake Keechelus Valley spread out at your feet, and beyond the rolling hills (with their many square scars of open clearcuts), the South Cascades sprawl to the horizon.

A half mile farther on, near the 3-mile mark, cross the road, which has flipped through a switchback turn and is now climbing south, and head straight up-slope to the ridge crest. Turn right and follow the crest to the 4,554-foot summit. A thin stand of trees lines the summit crest, providing a degree of protection from the wind while you enjoy a scenic lunch before heading down the steep slopes.

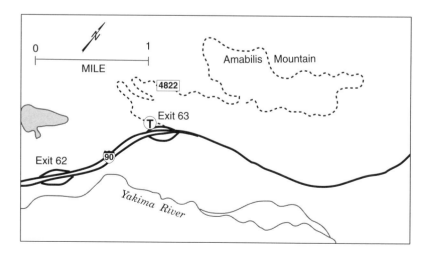

--*53*--

Thorp Mountain

Rating:	Backcountry
Round trip:	15 miles
Hiking time:	2 days
Elevation gain:	2,800 feet
High point:	5,100 feet
Best season:	Late December through March
Maps:	Green Trails: Kachess Lake No. 208
Who to contact:	Wenatchee National Forest, Cle Elum Ranger District

Thorp Mountain is one of the preeminent summer hiking trails in the area, but winter recreationists often overlook the beautiful peak because it requires a long snowshoe slog along a road before jumping on the narrow trail to the summit. Still, snowshoers who don't mind making camp in the snowy forest will find Thorp Mountain Trail to be extraordinarily beautiful and serene.

The route climbs steeply at times, along both the road and the trail, but generally the snowshoeing is easy. Because the trail is in the bottom of the creek valley most of the way, there are few panoramic views; but looking up-valley, Thorp Mountain captivates snowshoers working their way toward it, and the creek valley itself provides plenty of pretty scenery.

To get there, from Seattle drive east on Interstate 90 over Snoqualmie Pass to Exit 80, signed as Roslyn exit. Turn north onto the Bullfrog Cutoff Road, and drive to its end at a junction with State Route 903. Turn left and continue north 9 miles, passing through the towns of Roslyn and Ronald, to reach the junction with French Cabin Creek Road on the left, just past the Cle Elum River Campground. Park near the start of French Cabin Creek Road in wide plowed turnouts.

Start snowshoeing up French Cabin Creek Road as it crosses the Cle Elum River and ambles a quarter mile to the base of the valley wall. It then climbs steeply up the ridge on the north side of French Cabin Creek. The road stays above the creek basin for 1.5 miles, switching back time and again. Take advantage of the open terrain, and cut straight up the slope rather than rambling around the looping turns. Near 2 miles, the summit of Red Mountain is seen to the north. This mountain will remain in view

Using poles to help ascend the Thorp Mountain trail

much of the next mile, and at 3.4 miles, the road crosses Thorp Creek and comes to a junction with the Thorp Creek Road.

Turn right onto Thorp Creek Road (3,200 feet), and 1.5 miles up this road—5 miles from the start of the route—turn right to cross the creek and pick up the start of the narrow Thorp Mountain Trail. Consider pitching camp near here, so you can make an early morning start of the steep climb toward the summit of Thorp Mountain. If the avalanche danger is moderate or higher, this is the end of the trail, period. From this point on, there are some severe avalanche slopes.

The trail follows the north side of Thorp Creek up-valley for another mile, crossing through old pine forest, dense alder thickets, and the base of a major avalanche chute. At 6 miles, the trail is up against the head of the

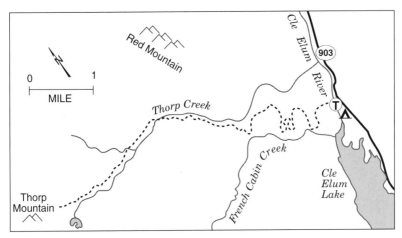

creek valley and the serious climbing begins. In the next 1.5 miles, the trail gains 1,600 feet to reach the 5,100-foot bench on the ridge below the summit of Thorp Mountain. The scramble to the true summit at 5,854 feet requires winter mountaineering skills. Better to stop at the ridge crest (if that is even attained) and enjoy the vistas offered there. Red Mountain, No Name Ridge, and West Peak tower all around, while the Cle Elum Lake Basin is nestled below to the east and Kachess Lake lies below to the west.

--54--

Hex Mountain

Rating:	More difficult
Round trip:	7 miles
Hiking time:	6 hours
Elevation gain:	2,600 feet
High point:	5,034 feet
Best season:	Late December through March
Maps:	Green Trails: Kachess Lake No. 208
Who to contact:	Wenatchee National Forest, Cle Elum Ranger District
	See page 166 for map.

This trail represents the epitome of snowshoeing in the Cascades: a long, steady, often-steep climb through lush old forests ending at a high ridge with panoramic views of unmatched beauty. After soaking in the scenic splendor at the summit, snowshoers then reverse direction and follow their tracks back down the slope.

What sets this trail apart from others is that the slopes are well forested and sheltered, so avalanche hazards are minimal and snowshoeing, though steep at times, is relatively easy. Starting from Salmon la Sac Road (State Route 903), the snowshoe hike begins with a climb on an old, winding logging road through mixed forest and small clearcuts. Some nice views are found on the way up the trail, but the best are left until snowshoers top the ridge and turn around to see the breathtaking vistas to the west. Cle Elum Lake sprawls directly underfoot, and just beyond that is Mount Baldy, Thomas Mountain, West Peak, and Thorp Mountain along the crest of Kachess Ridge.

To get there, from Seattle drive east on Interstate 90 over Snoqualmie Pass to Exit 80, signed as Roslyn exit. Turn north onto the Bullfrog Cutoff Road, and drive to its end at a junction with State Route 903. Turn left and continue north 9 miles, passing through the towns of Roslyn and Ronald, to reach the junction of Forest Service Road No. 116 on the right. If a turnout is plowed out here, park in it; otherwise, go back down State Route 903 about 300 yards to a plowed area on the west side of the highway near where it crosses Newport Creek.

If you park at Newport Creek, walk up the highway to Road No. 116 before strapping on your snowshoes and starting the climb. The road leads northeast, always climbing, past several spur roads and side trails. Most of these are easily discernible as secondary roads, but at times the forks and junctions can be confusing. Unfortunately, trying to map all the junctions and byways is difficult, so you will have to use your best judgment and occasionally backtrack if you make a wrong turn. (Fortunately, the side roads are generally short, so you'll quickly realize your errors. For example, if the road dips or heads too far off the northeast bearing that is required, it's the wrong road.)

After the first mile of the road, the options decrease and the main road is the only one to follow until, at 1.2 miles, the road traverses above a small creek valley and, at 1.7 miles, ends at the summer trailhead parking area. Here is where the fun really begins. Snowshoeing up the narrow forest trail as it climbs the ridge crest toward Hex Mountain is a wonderful experience. With snowshoes you can easily climb, weave around trees, and generally enjoy the day as you soak in the beauty of the forest environment. This area is home to red foxes and an assortment of birds and small animals. Of course, whiskey jacks pester every human who enters the forest, thus living

Foggy day on the Hex Mountain trail

up to their alias, camp-robber jays, and great-horned owls silently patrol the woods in search of mice, voles, martens, and hares.

The trail climbs for over a mile and a half with only occasional glimpses of the world beyond the trees. At 3.3 miles from the start of the hike, the trail tops out on the south end of Sasse Ridge, just below the summit of Hex Mountain. Turn right onto the Sasse Ridge Trail, and hike a quarter mile to the summit for striking views of the eastern Cascades.

--55--

Sasse Ridge

Rating:	Backcountry
Round trip:	15.4 miles
Hiking time:	2 days
Elevation gain:	2,700 feet
High point:	5,400 feet
Best season:	Late December through March
Maps:	Green Trails: Kachess Lake No. 208
Who to contact:	Wenatchee National Forest, Cle Elum Ranger District
	See page 166 for map.

After a modest climb to the ridge crest, this route lets snowshoers stay high and enjoy an endless bounty of beautiful views and remarkable scenery. The trail rolls south to north and opens up on views of the Alpine Lakes Wilderness peaks, Cle Elum Lake, and the entire eastern Cascade Mountains.

Few folks visit the north end of this trail in winter, so those snowshoers who do venture out along the route will find it empty of human company. Still, they won't be alone. A host of wintering animals thrive here, including a few who perform chameleon acts by changing into snowy white coats each winter. Snowshoe hares, ptarmigans, and weasels are seen as flashes of white against the white snow only when they move. But even their winter camouflage can't save them from the predators who prowl this area. Coyotes, bobcats, cougars, red-tailed hawks, golden eagles, falcons, and great-horned owls all compete for the few small animals that scamper about the snowy forests and meadows of Sasse Ridge.

To get there, from Seattle drive east on Interstate 90 over Snoqualmie Pass to Exit 80, signed as Roslyn exit. Turn north onto the Bullfrog Cutoff

Heading toward Sasse Mountain along the ridge crest

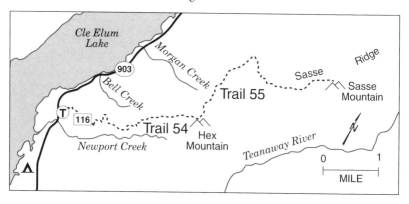

Road, and drive to its end at a junction with State Route 903. Turn left and continue north 9 miles, passing through the towns of Roslyn and Ronald, to reach the junction of Forest Service Road No. 116 on the right. If a turnout is plowed out here, park in it; otherwise, go back down Route 903 about 300 yards to a plowed area on the west side of the highway near where it crosses Newport Creek.

Start up Road No. 116 as described in the Hex Mountain Trail. At the top of the trail, at 3.3 miles, instead of turning right for a short scramble to the summit of Hex, turn left onto the Sasse Ridge Trail and start the long, scenic snowshoe north. The trail follows the crest of the ridge for more than 7 miles, but you can find plenty of fine, protected campsites all along the route, so tailor the length of the snowshoe trek to your own preferences.

From the 4,900-foot junction with the Hex Mountain Trail, the Sasse Ridge Trail heads north, dropping gradually through thin forests in the first mile before climbing once more until, at 5.3 miles, the trail rolls under the crown of a high, unnamed peak (5,159 feet). The trail then banks right, drops slightly into a high saddle, and climbs again to 5,400 feet at 5.8 miles. Wind exposure and potential avalanche dangers are possible on this stretch of the trail. If conditions are unstable, head back and make camp in the first sheltered site, either near the saddle or on the south side of the unnamed peak.

The trail curves north again at 5.9 miles and at 7.5 passes just under the summit of Sasse Mountain. The scramble to the summit is easy because the peak is open and round. Enjoy unmatched views from the top of Sasse, and either find a suitable campsite in the thin forests on the mountain's protected southern flank or head back down the trail to find a sheltered camp.

North of Sasse Mountain, the trail crosses a steep, open ridge section that is a dangerous avalanche area. The wind-swept ridge is seldom stable or secure, so only highly experienced winter mountaineers should even consider going farther, and they should do so only when avalanche dangers are low.

--*56*--
Salmon la Sac Creek

Rating:	Most difficult
Round trip:	6.4 miles
Hiking time:	5 hours
Elevation gain:	1,300 feet
High point:	4,700 feet
Best season:	Late December through March
Maps:	Green Trails: Kachess Lake No. 208
Who to contact:	Wenatchee National Forest, Cle Elum Ranger District

A number of good trails lead out of the Salmon la Sac area, but this is one of the few that is almost completely ignored by snowmobilers and skiers, leaving it for snowshoers to explore in quiet solitude. The trail rolls east, climbing gradually through pretty ponderosa pine and larch forest. The forest shelters the trail for most of its length, but there are enough openings in the canopy to provide some nice views of the Cle Elum River Basin and the mountains beyond. Between those panoramic peeks, the sparkling little creek and snow-swaddled forest offer all the scenic diversion any snowshoer could want.

To get there, from Seattle drive east on Interstate 90 over Snoqualmie Pass to Exit 80, signed as Roslyn exit. Turn north onto the Bullfrog Cutoff Road, and drive to its end at a junction with State Route 903. Turn left, and continue north 9 miles, passing through the towns of Roslyn and Ronald, to the end of the plowed road at the Salmon la Sac Picnic Area and Sno-Park.

The trail leaves the Salmon la Sac area from behind the Cayuse Horse Camp facilities. Follow the signs for Trail No. 1307. The path weaves through the trees, climbing gradually for the first half mile before finally traversing south to the Salmon la Sac Creek Basin. The creek is a tiny rivulet that sparkles and splashes along its ice-laden banks, providing a pretty picture for winter recreationists.

The trail becomes steep, and for the next mile, it climbs ruthlessly through a long series of switchbacks, staying high above the creek. At 1.6 miles, the trail levels somewhat and begins a long, climbing traverse into the creek basin, crossing the creek at 2.7 miles (4,300 feet) and following it

another half mile to a trail junction at 4,700 feet. This is a good turnaround point. If you have plenty of energy and daylight left, follow the right fork for another mile to a bench below the summit of Jolly Mountain.

This trail climbs steeply toward its end, however, and a few avalanche chutes should keep you away any time the avalanche danger is moderate or higher. The left fork at the junction is steep and slide-prone much of the time, so avoid it at all times.

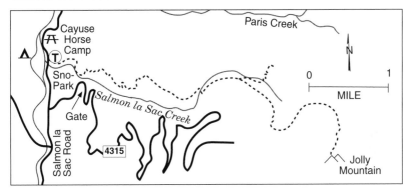

--57--

Cooper River

Rating: More difficult
Round trip: 8 miles
Hiking time: 6 hours
Elevation gain: 400 feet
High point: 2,900 feet
Best season: Late December through March
Maps: Green Trails: Kachess Lake No. 208
Who to contact: Wenatchee National Forest, Cle Elum Ranger District

Thank goodness the Salmon la Sac area has plenty of roads because they keep the snowmobilers off quiet trails like this one that parallels Cooper River upstream to Cooper Lake. This route is occasionally used by cross-country skiers, but more often than not, snowshoers will find they have the wide, pretty trail all to themselves.

The trail is relatively flat, and finding the route is not difficult, even in

Pausing to enjoy the view

Stones and snow along the Cooper River

heavy snow years, because the trail corridor is wide and nearly straight. Snowshoers can enjoy their surroundings here as they stroll up the path, gazing in wonder at the beautiful snow-shrouded landscape. The forest is a mixed bag of old pine and fir, so it is generally open and light. Sun streaks in through the thin canopy to keep the valley bright and sunny. Deer are frequently seen in this valley, even in winter, and many small birds and animals can be seen along the trail as well. Kids and adults alike will enjoy studying and trying to identify the many animal tracks left in the snow beside the trail and along the riverbanks.

To get there, from Seattle drive east on Interstate 90 over Snoqualmie Pass to Exit 80, signed as Roslyn exit. Turn north onto the Bullfrog Cutoff Road, and drive to its end at a junction with State Route 903. Turn left and continue north 9 miles, passing through the towns of Roslyn and Ronald, to the end of the plowed road at the Salmon la Sac Picnic Area and Sno-Park.

Snowshoe up the road past the ranger station, and cross the river toward the Salmon la Sac Campground. The trail is well signed and easy to find. Stay right, and snowshoe up a small service road. The trailhead is located on this road, about 200 feet past the gated entrance to the campground. The trail stays alongside, but not too near, Cooper River for its entire length. If you have difficulty finding the trail—especially in the first half mile—just head northeast, keeping the river off to your left, but no more than 50 or 60 yards away.

The first half mile is in fairly open, airy forest, so the snow piles deep and obscures landmarks and trail tread. Beyond this section, the route is easy to find. The wide corridor skirts the bottom edge of the Polallie Ridge wall where it meets the Cooper River Valley bottom. The views, while not amazing, are quite picturesque. In addition to the scenic river views, you can catch occasional glimpses up the valley of Polallie Ridge on the right and Chikamin Ridge straight ahead.

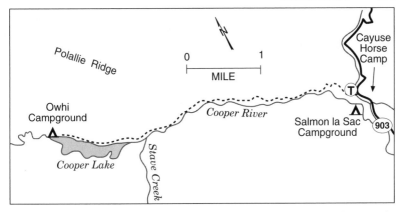

The valley narrows considerably after the first half mile, and at 1 mile, the trail is squeezed tight into a narrow gorge. The river quickens, and the trail climbs until, at 2 miles, it levels out and the valley opens up again. The walls stay close, but not nearly as confining as the section just passed. The last 1.5 miles of trail ramble gently and serenely to a junction with Forest Service Road No. 4616 along the banks of Cooper Lake. To see the lake, and enjoy a lunch spot with pretty views of the lake and the high ridges around it, turn right onto the road and hike up a few hundred yards to catch the Lake Shore Trail on the left. Drop down along this trail, and skirt the lake to any one of a dozen good viewpoints and picnic areas. Owhi Campground is just a half mile up the lakeshore if a larger lunch spot is needed.

--58--
Indian Creek

Rating:	Easiest to more difficult
Round trip:	Up to 14 miles
Hiking time:	2 to 10 hours
Elevation gain:	1,300 feet
High point:	3,600 feet
Best season:	Late December through March
Maps:	Green Trails: Mount Stuart No. 209
Who to contact:	Wenatchee National Forest, Cle Elum Ranger District

Many individual mountains in Washington are extremely beautiful, but no range of peaks is more spectacular than the long, jagged line of

Tracks in thin snow, Teanaway/Indian Creek route

mountains of the Stuart Range. This route lets snowshoers gaze in awe at the impressive summits as they amble up the wide Teanaway Valley. The pretty Wenatchee Mountains, a lower, less spectacular range, provide a picturesque foreground for the more massive Stuarts behind.

Because of the wonderful views, not to mention the beautiful forest and river environments of the Teanaway Valley itself, this area gets a lot of winter visitors. Snowshoers will find the road well traveled by skiers and snowmobilers, as well as other snowshoers. The route described here lets

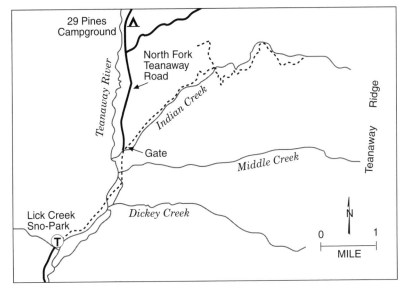

snowshoers enjoy the views, while tolerating the crowds, before climbing a side valley that is much quieter and less visited. Indian Creek Road climbs the deep basin of the creek, but the road ends before the valley does. That, and the fact that the Stuart Range isn't visible from the valley, keeps most snowmobilers out of the basin, and skiers prefer the more scenic valleys farther up the Teanaway. Snowshoers might consider these other routes, too, but since skiers can travel faster on the flat Teanaway Road, they beat the 'shoers to the viewpoints. So Indian Creek Valley is the snowshoers' best bet for a Teanaway trek.

To get there, from Seattle drive east on Interstate 90 over Snoqualmie Pass to Exit 85 and turn north onto State Route 970. Drive 5 miles before turning left (northwest) onto Teanaway Road (Forest Service Road No. 9737). About 7 miles up the valley, when the road (and river) splits, stay right on the North Fork Teanaway Road and continue 2 miles to the end of the plowed road at a wide Sno-Park facility.

Start up the North Fork Teanaway Road as it curves northeast alongside the pretty Teanaway River. Stop to enjoy the meadows along the river bottom by stepping off the road now and again and ambling out across the open snow for close-up looks at the river. Or head off into the stands of trees that separate the many meadows, keeping a close eye out for small birds and animals that thrive in these protected woods.

The valley slowly hooks north, gradually revealing more and more of the snow-capped rocks of the high Stuart Range. The road crosses the river at about 1.5 miles, and at about the 2-mile mark, the road and the valley it climbs in are pointed due north. This is where Mount Stuart bursts onto the horizon. The western end of the staggeringly beautiful Stuart Range is anchored by this mountain—a high, near-vertical wall of rock and ice. In front of the great range lies the lesser but also beautiful Wenatchee Mountain Range. The peaks along this front are less dramatic—no vertical walls of granite here—but they are high enough, and craggy enough, to provide an outstanding foreground to the towering Stuarts in the background. Together, the two ranges create a perfect picture, so make sure to bring along a camera and lots of film.

At 3 miles, just after crossing Indian Creek, find the Indian Creek Road angling off to the right. A gate across the bottom of the road—and the fact that the road dead-ends in a few miles—keeps snowmobilers out. Hike up the little-used road, crossing meadows, clearcuts, and deep forests for up to 4 more miles before turning back. A half mile up the valley, all views of the Stuarts are cut off, but Indian Creek is a pretty little stream, and the snowbound valley is a fun playground. Enjoy this route for its own sake rather than for the rewards at trail's end because, on this trail, the rewards are found along its length.

--59--
Sun Top

Rating:	More difficult
Round trip:	9.5 miles
Hiking time:	7.5 hours
Elevation gain:	3,000 feet
High point:	5,280 feet
Best season:	Early January through late February
Maps:	Green Trails: Greenwater No. 238
Who to contact:	Mount Baker–Snoqualmie National Forest, White River Ranger District

The route to the top of Sun Top is often groomed for cross-country skiers, but snowshoers will still enjoy this trek. After all, the views are just as spectacular, and the winter landscape just as pretty, even when the trail has

Rime ice coats a tree near the summit of Sun Top

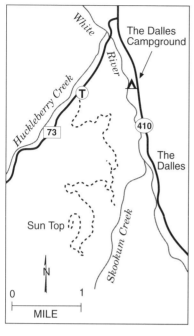

been leveled for skiers. Just stick to the edges of the trail to avoid tromping on the tracks, and take advantage of any opportunity to climb off the trail and cross open meadows for maximum snowshoeing fun.

Attaining the summit of Sun Top requires considerable energy, but the workout is well rewarded with unmatched views of the country northwest of Mount Rainier. The White River Valley stretches below the mountain, and Mount Rainier towers above. The lower section of the trail is sometimes visited by the White River elk herd, so keep an eye out for the big beasts. This is also prime cougar country (due, in large part, to the presence of the elk herd). Seeing one of the big cats is a pleasure. Cougars pose little threat to adult humans, although kids shouldn't be allowed to run ahead. The odds of seeing a mountain lion are extremely low, but a couple lucky snowshoers have excitedly reported seeing the tawny cats streaking away from the trail when the elk are nearby.

To get there, from Enumclaw drive east on State Route 410 for 24 miles and turn right (south) onto Forest Service Road No. 73 (Huckleberry Creek). Drive south 1.5 miles to the Sun Top Sno-Park.

The route to the summit follows Forest Service Road No. 7315. Snowshoe up the only road leaving the Sno-Park, pass the gate, and in a couple hundred feet, turn left up Road No. 7315. The road climbs steadily to the summit, and because of the frequent clearcuts encountered along the hike, there are ample opportunities to stop, rest, and savor the scenery spread out before you. As the trail climbs the ridge line, look down into the wide White River Valley and the narrower, darker Huckleberry Basin. The best place to find elk is along the lower clearcuts, although from the higher clearcuts it's possible to look down into the open meadows along the rivers. Using a good pair of binoculars, scan the river meadows for the large herds that live in the White River drainage.

A few spur roads are found along the way, and these make nice diversions from the well-traveled main road. Snowshoe out along them for a new view, and then angle up through the trees and meadows to rejoin the main trail. By climbing straight through the larger clearcuts rather than following the looping trail, you can save nearly a mile and enjoy some untracked snow.

Following the road all the way, it is 5 miles to a high bench below the summit of Sun Top. The summit approach requires crossing some serious avalanche slopes, so attempt the top only when conditions are stable and avalanche dangers reported as low. For the best views south to Rainier, angle southwest around the bench about 400 yards to an open view of Mount Rainier and all the lesser peaks between.

--60--

Bullion Basin

Rating:	Backcountry
Round trip:	4.5 miles
Hiking time:	4 hours
Elevation gain:	1,500 feet
High point:	5,800 feet
Best season:	Early December through early March
Maps:	Green Trails: Bumping Lake No. 271
Who to contact:	Mount Baker–Snoqualmie National Forest, White River Ranger District

Snowshoers flock to this trail on winter weekends, but there is something unusual about a lot of the snowshoers here. Many of them have long planks strapped to their backs as they ascend the steep trail. These are cross-over 'shoers. They use their shoes to get them to the top of steep, deep slopes and then trade their snowshoes for snowboards and swoosh down the smooth slopes. Even nonboarding snowshoers will appreciate the artistry these backcountry snowboarders exhibit on their downhill runs.

But Bullion Basin has a lot more to offer than just the chance to watch some backcountry thrill-seekers shred powder. This trail has high, sub-alpine meadows blanketed in deep snow, wonderful views of the surrounding craggy peaks, and an array of destination options to assure solitude for those who want it. The trail climbs steeply, and there are some serious avalanche slopes around the area, so snowshoers here need to be ready for a workout and must know how to recognize and avoid avalanche dangers.

But when the conditions are stable, this is a wonderful winter world to explore and experience.

To get there, from Enumclaw drive east on State Route 410 to the end of the plowed highway and turn left onto Crystal Mountain Road (Forest Service Road No. 7190). Continue up this winding road to the Crystal Mountain Ski Area. Park in the upper parking lot if space is available. The ski area asks that backcountry travelers sign in with the ski patrol so they can account for any cars left in the lot after the lifts close down.

The route follows Trail No. 1156 east toward Blue Bell Pass. The trailhead is found to the east (left, as you face the ski slopes) side of the ski area parking lot, behind the condominiums and buildings on the hillside. From the upper end of the parking lot, angle left up the steep slope, skirting the beginners' slope at the base of the valley wall. Snowshoeing along the tree line, find an old roadway and more skier cabins. A small ski lift on the right ends near the road—stay well to the left of it to the first switchback on the narrow road. The trail sign should be visible at this switchback in all but the heaviest snow years.

Trail No. 1156 climbs left along a traverse across the slope to 5,000 feet, and then switches back a few times before settling in for a long climb up the small Bullion Creek draw. If the trail is drifted over and difficult to find, simply pick a route along the north side of the creek and, in just over 1.5 miles, traverse right to cross the creek (near 5,600 feet). Hike through a thin stand of forest, climbing straight up the slope above to reach

The view from Crystal Mountain Ski Area, Bullion Basin route

the open meadows of Bullion Basin at 5,800 feet.

Plenty of variations are available on the approach route, but generally, evaluate the slopes and find a path as near to the actual route of the summer hiking trail as possible while steering clear of the steep slide-prone slopes. Lots of open country is found along the way, so views are spectacular all the way up. From Bullion Basin enjoy views of the ski area as well as of the snowboarders playing nearby. If

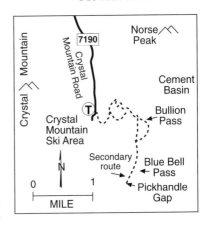

you are the adventurous sort, choose to scramble another mile (gaining some 600 feet) up steep slopes to the ridge crest at Blue Bell Pass. However, Bullion Basin is so pretty and scenic, there is really no need to go any higher in your explorations. Scramble around the basin to find a nice, quiet picnic spot, enjoy a leisurely meal, and then head back down.

--61--
Mowich Lake

Rating: Easiest
Round trip: 10 miles
Hiking time: 6 hours
Elevation gain: 1,400 feet
High point: 5,000 feet
Best season: Early December through late March
Maps: Green Trails: Mount Rainier West No. 269
Who to contact: Mount Rainier National Park
See page 184 for map.

Mowich Lake is the destination of choice for most folks who want to play on the northwest side of Mount Rainier National Park. The road is closed at the park boundary shortly after the first heavy snowfall, and the 5.5-mile trip to the lakeshore is a favorite of skiers and snowshoers who want to enjoy the beauty of the park, without working too hard at their sports. The road is steep in places, but overall it is moderately sloped and

wide enough for snowshoers and skiers to enjoy together.

Snowshoers will find themselves climbing through lush, old cedar forests—some truly massive trees are found in this area—and thinner stands of fir and hemlock before arriving at the lake with its views of Tolmie Peak, Paul Peak, and Mount Rainier. The lake has an array of excellent campsites, each well-sheltered but with great views all around. The gentle road hike in makes this a good destination for novice winter campers as well as seasoned cold-weather fanatics.

To get there, from Enumclaw drive 5 miles west on State Route 410 to the small town of Buckley and, on the west end of town, turn left (south) onto State Route 165. Continue for 10 miles through the communities of Carbonado and Wilkeson before crossing the one-lane bridge over the deep Fairfax Gorge on the Carbon River. Just beyond the bridge, turn right onto Mowich Lake Road (Forest Service Road No. 79)—a narrow road that climbs through a clearcut slope. Drive 11 miles to the national park boundary or to the snow line. Park along the road, leaving the roadway clear so that other vehicles can pass and turn around safely.

From the gate at the park boundary (3,000 feet), hike up the road as it skirts around the flank of Martin Peak and climbs gradually up the Meadow Creek Valley, passing the Paul Peak Trail at 1 mile. The thick tree cover is broken by an occasional small clearing, but dense, ancient forests dominate the first 2 miles of the route. At this point, the road rolls through the Mowich Meadows—small fields of snow nestled among the trees. The road curves right past the meadows and climbs steeply for a few hundred yards, rolling south through a sweeping curve. At 3 miles, rather than following the road down through a roundabout course, find a small trail on the left and climb steeply for a quarter mile to rejoin the road at 4,400 feet, thus trimming more than a half mile off the distance to the lake.

Instead of rejoining the wandering road at the junction, cross the road and start up another trail as it climbs steeply to the south, cutting across the neck of a long northerly loop in the road. A half mile up this trail, at 3.8 miles, cross the road once more and stay on the small forest trail as it continues to angle up the slope on a southern bearing. This half-mile trail cuts nearly a mile off the road distance. Road hikers will sweep west with the road as it rounds a sharp switchback and returns.

Back on the road at mile 4.3, turn left and hike a half mile to the east to find Mowich Lake. Once at the lakeshore, turn right and follow the road along the shoreline to a flat area at the end of the road. Tolmie Peak is

Mount Rainier from Mowich Lake Road

visible to the north from here. To see Mount Rainier, hike a quarter mile south to a viewpoint on the ridge above the lake. A small, level area for campers is nearby, with plenty of places for picnickers to plop down and enjoy lunch while gazing at the stony north face of the mighty mountain.

--*62*--
Paul Peak

Rating:	Most difficult
Round trip:	5.6 miles
Hiking time:	6.5 hours
Elevation gain:	1,800 feet
High point:	4,800 feet
Best season:	Early December through late March
Maps:	Green Trails: Mount Rainier West No. 269
Who to contact:	Mount Rainier National Park

Although this trail is within Mount Rainier National Park, no views of the big mountain are visible along this route. In fact, there are no sweeping panoramic views at all. Plenty of beautiful local scenery surrounds this trail, though, including a sparkling forest stream and lush old-growth forests that have stood here for eons. Quiet solitude is also a feature of this often-overlooked winter trail.

To get there, from Enumclaw drive 5 miles west on State Route 410 to the small town of Buckley and, on the west end of town, turn left (south) onto State Route 165. Continue 10 miles through the communities of Carbonado and Wilkeson before crossing the one-lane bridge over the deep Fairfax Gorge on the Carbon River. Just beyond the bridge, turn right onto Mowich Lake Road (Forest Service No. 79)—a narrow road that climbs through a clearcut slope. Drive 11 miles to the National Park boundary or to the snow line. Park along the road, leaving the roadway clear so that other vehicles can pass and turn around safely.

Start hiking up the Mowich Lake Road as it gradually climbs through deep old-growth forest. In a mile, turn right onto the well-signed Paul Peak Trail and drop a couple hundred feet in the next half mile until the trail crosses the beautiful Meadow Creek at 3,450 feet. The bridge over the creek is narrow and can be hazardous when snow-covered. If footing is too insecure, it might be necessary to slip out of your snowshoes and, using

Tracks of a snowshoe hare lead to a burrow under a cedar tree

trekking poles for balance, stomp a narrow track across the center of the bridge wearing just your boots.

The trail stays fairly level from the creek crossing, following the hillside south another half mile before curving east along the flank of Paul Peak. At 2.8 miles (3,500 feet), the trail suddenly turns south again and drops into a long set of switchbacks. Rather than following the trail down, turn around here and return the way you came for a modest, quiet outing. For a more energetic trip, angle up the slope above the trail. Traversing northwest, climb the slope above the trail, and near the 4,000-foot level, turn northeast and angle up a small ridge line toward the forested summit of Paul Peak.

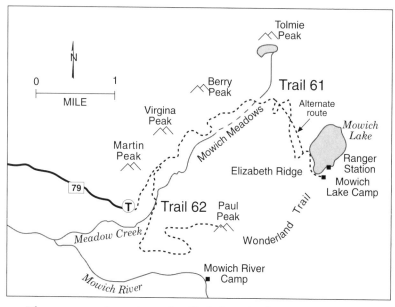

There are no views along the climb, but the forest is a wonderful example of mixed old growth, with cedar, Douglas fir, and hemlock and a few bigleaf-maples tossed in for good measure. Camp-robber jays, ptarmigans, grouse, hares, red foxes, coyotes, and cougars patrol the area. Best of all, few other snowshoers or other recreationists intrude on a quiet communion with nature in this popular national park.

--63--

Mount Beljica

Rating: More difficult
Round trip: 5.4 miles
Hiking time: 4 hours
Elevation gain: 900 feet
High point: 5,700 feet
Best season: December through early April
Maps: Green Trails: Mount Rainier West No. 269
Who to contact: Mount Rainier National Park

This trail starts off the Mount Tahoma Scenic *Ski* Trails, but there is no reason snowshoers can't use the trail—making sure they stay well clear of

Heavy snow blankets the trees near the summit of Mount Beljica

the ski tracks—to access the backcountry trail leading to the top of Mount Beljica. This narrow path weaves through thick forests and meadows, passes a pretty lake basin, and finally arrives at the summit of the low mountain on the western edge of Mount Rainier National Park. The peak is not a towering summit, but it does provide some incredible views of Mount Rainier and the peaks to the southwest, including Eagle and Chutla Peaks at the western end of the Tatoosh Range.

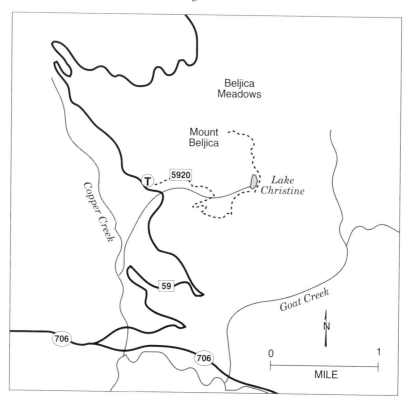

Snowshoers will find that the route is gentle and easy to follow, offering novice and intermediate snowshoers a chance to experience backcountry travel without having to deal with steep climbs and tricky routefinding problems. However, this is a backcountry route rather than a simple road walk, so everyone should have basic skills in routefinding, avalanche awareness and recognition, and winter survival techniques.

To get there, drive east from Tacoma on State Route 7 to Elbe and turn left onto State Route 706—the Road to Paradise—and continue east to Ashford. Drive 3.5 miles past the town limits, and turn left (north) onto Forest Service Road No. 59 (signed as the Northern Section of the Mount Tahoma Trail System). Drive 5 miles on the steep, narrow road (traction tires required, chains recommended) to the Sno-Park.

From the Sno-Park, snowshoe on the right on Forest Service Road No. 5920 as it climbs up a steep valley. (Most of the ski traffic will be going straight ahead on Road No. 59 toward the Mount Tahoma hut system.) In a mile, the road crosses a small stream, and for the next half mile, it rolls steeply upward through a series of switchbacks flanked by dense stands of second-growth forest. At the end of the road, 1.5 miles from the Sno-Park, is the start of the Mount Beljica Hiking Trail. This trail climbs gradually around the flank of a small ridge and crosses into the Glacier View Wilderness Area at 2.2 miles, just before climbing into the Lake Christine Basin. Now in wilderness, the trail weaves through older, more mature forest as it turns north along a small ridge leading to the south flank of Mount Beljica. It's a flat half mile from the north shore of Lake Christine to the eastern flank of the mountain.

The mountain will slowly rise to your left. Pick a clear route through the forest and meadows, angling left (northwest) to the 5,475-foot summit for good views of Mount Rainier and the lesser peaks flanking it.

--64--

Kautz Creek

Rating:	More difficult
Round trip:	Up to 11 miles
Hiking time:	7 hours
Elevation gain:	2,800 feet
High point:	5,300 feet
Best season:	January through early March
Maps:	Green Trails: Mount Rainier West No. 269
Who to contact:	Mount Rainier National Park

Kautz Creek offers not only an excellent snowshoe excursion but also a chance to experience the geologic history of Mount Rainier. The trail climbs along the route followed by mudflows, lahars, and floods that date back tens of thousands of years. Lest one think that is all ancient history, bear in mind that the last massive mudflow in this valley occurred in 1947 when some 50 million cubic yards of mud, water, and debris flashed through the valley, burying the Road to Paradise and killing most of the trees in the lower valley bottom. A forest of silver snags is what remains today. But the picture isn't all that bleak. Although the valley is routinely the scene of geologic destruction, the area is awash in beauty between those catastrophic events. This route follows the tumultuous creek, then climbs through ancient forests, and finally rolls through wide, open meadows with spectacular views.

Wet, sticky snow on the windward side of trees—an indication of avalanche danger

To get there, drive east from Tacoma on State Route 7 and bear right onto State Route 706 at the town of Elbe. Continue east through the Nisqually Entrance of the park, and proceed 3 miles farther to the parking area on the right just beyond the Kautz Creek Bridge. The trail begins on the north side of the road.

The trail is wide and easy to follow. The early section may be thinly covered in snow some years, so you might have to begin the outing with your snowshoes attached to your pack instead of your feet. However, the trail climbs steadily, and the snow is generally deep enough to require snow-shoes well before the footbridge is reached at the 1-mile mark. Check with a ranger before heading out in early spring to make sure this bridge is in-tact: spring floods sometimes wash it away. Exercise caution when crossing the bridge. The snow accumulated on it tends to pile up at an angle, so the first person across should take his or her time and kick out good, solid footpads for those following. It may be necessary to remove your snow-shoes to increase your stability when crossing.

Once over the creek, the trail begins to climb the valley wall, angling up through the forest between Tumtum Peak and Satulick Mountain. You can catch occasional peeks at these summits as you climb. The climb be-gins as a gradual straight-on pitch, and then turns into steep switchbacks. Around the 4,000-foot level, the trail swings into a long hillside traverse around the head of a small creek valley (a tributary to Pyramid Creek), followed by another series of switchbacks. At 4 miles from your car, the route enters the first long, broad meadow. Views south to the Kautz Valley and north to the glacier-covered flank of Mount Rainier are found here. This makes an excellent place to have lunch and turn around. If you prefer an extended adventure, carefully climb through the meadow and a tricky

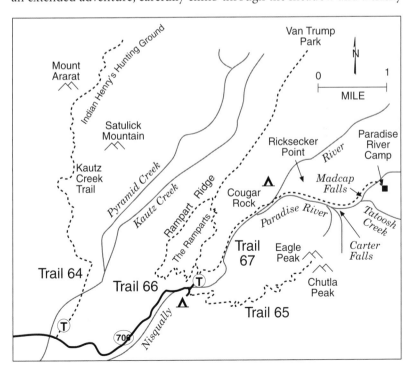

traverse through another clearing in the next mile before finding a long half-mile traverse around the flank of Mount Ararat to reach the beginning of Indian Henry's Hunting Ground.

--*65*--
Eagle and Chutla Peaks Trail

Rating:	Most difficult
Round trip:	7 miles
Hiking time:	6 hours
Elevation gain:	2,900 feet
High point:	5,600 feet
Best season:	January through early March
Maps:	Green Trails: Mount Rainier West No. 269
Who to contact:	Mount Rainier National Park

See page 189 for map.

Climbing through mossy old-growth forest, this trail ascends the western flank of the Tatoosh Range. The trail is quiet and often overlooked by snowshoers—it is often overlooked by summer hikers as well—but it offers an excellent opportunity to get out and enjoy the wonders of a winter woodland environment. Not to mention a chance to interact with an array of wildlife, including the ever-present camp-robber jays (a.k.a. gray jays or whiskey jacks), red foxes, bobcats, and blacktail deer. A flash of white movement seen in the snowy forest could be a ptarmigan, a weasel, or a snowshoe hare, all of which trade in their brown summer coverings for white winter coats.

To get there, drive east from Tacoma on State Route 7 and bear right onto State Route 706 at the town of Elbe. Continue east through the Nisqually Entrance of the park, and proceed to Longmire Ranger Station and Lodge. Park in the plowed area behind the lodge.

The route begins with a hike up the service road behind the ranger station, passing the employee housing area and crossing the Nisqually River via a narrow one-lane bridge. Continue up the road 100 yards to the trailhead on the left. In low snow years, you may not need your snowshoes for the first half mile or so; but even when the snow is relatively shallow, snowshoes can be helpful on the trail with their sure-grip cleats and crampons.

The route climbs through a couple of moderate switchbacks, each followed by long traverses across the hillside, before entering a series of increasingly short switchbacks in the shady forest. The trail is always climbing, but never too steeply. At 2 miles, the trail crosses a tiny creek—the stream it has followed up the hillside for the previous mile.

The forest around the trail is thick, and the trail rolls through an endless series of tree wells and snow mounds. These features form when a large opening in the forest canopy allows more snow to reach the ground, piling it deeper than that under the trees. The walking isn't overly difficult, but the constant up-and-down motion does make the walking slow. But this is a trail to be savored and enjoyed, not rushed through. The broad canopy and forest of ancient trees is worth experiencing. Stop and listen to the birds. Smell the wet cedars. Feel the sun as it streams through openings in the canopy, and taste the water as it drips off the fir limbs and onto your face. At just over 3 miles, near the 3.25-mile mark, the trail enters a sidehill meadow. This clearing provides good views of Eagle and Chutla Peaks ahead. If snow conditions allow it, continue up through this meadow to reach Eagle Saddle—between Eagle and Chutla Peaks—for vistas that sweep over Mount Rainier, Tumtum Peak, Eagle and Chutla Peaks as well as the rest of the Tatoosh Range. On very clear days, the top of Mount Adams may be seen peeking up on the southeastern horizon.

--66--

Rampart Ridge

Rating:	More difficult
Round trip:	4.5 miles
Hiking time:	5 hours
Elevation gain:	1,200 feet
High point:	4,050 feet
Best season:	January through early March
Maps:	Green Trails: Mount Rainier West No. 269
Who to contact:	Mount Rainier National Park
	See page 189 for map.

This is a forest trek through ancient cedars and firs, with panoramic views of the wide Nisqually Valley and nearby peaks. There are also occasional glimpses of the snowy face of Mount Rainier, but the real beauty of this

route is the wonderful local scenery. The deep old-growth forest is home to an assortment of birds and animals, including ravens, red foxes, and snowshoe hares. Because it is on the lower flanks of the mountain, this trail gets its snow later than the routes near Paradise. But once the big winter storms of January and February hit, Rampart Ridge is an excellent option, especially on those days when the Road to Paradise stays gated at Longmire well into late morning. The route is a loop trip which is best when hiked clockwise from Longmire Lodge, as there are gentler slopes to climb this way.

To get there, drive east from Tacoma on State Route 7 and bear right onto State Route 706 at the town of Elbe. Continue east through the Nisqually Entrance of the park, and proceed to Longmire Ranger Station and Lodge. Park in the plowed area behind the lodge, and find the start of the trail in the meadows across the road.

The snowshoe hike begins on the well-marked Trail of the Shadows nature walk. Go left on this small loop trail, and in just a few hundred yards, bear left again, leaving the meadow and starting up a wide, well-signed trail (Rampart Ridge Trail) into the trees. Even under deep snow, the trail is easy to follow through the woods. Continue upward, weaving between the mammoth old trees as the trail goes from one wide switchback to another. In 2 miles, you'll reach the crest of the ridge and open views to the west of Nisqually Valley and the cone-shaped Tumtum Peak. A short bit beyond, you pass the high point of the route, and look down over the cliffs that give the ridge its name—The Ramparts. From here it's a relatively flat mile of forest hiking, with occasional meadows and views of Rainier, before reaching a trail junction. The cross trail is the Wonderland Trail.

If you want a bit more adventure, and a few more clear looks at the mountain, go straight to continue along the upper reaches of Rampart Ridge. The trail leads another 2.5 miles to Van Trump Park, gaining another 1,500 feet along the way. This extension would increase your round-trip mileage to nearly 10 miles.

To close the loop, go right at the junction with the Wonderland Trail and descend through a long series of switchbacks, slicing through thick forest along the way. The final half mile of the trail is pretty much a gentle straight shot back to the road, just above Longmire. Hike the last 100 yards west along the shoulder of the Road to Paradise to reach the Longmire Lodge area.

The view to the southeast from Rampart Ridge

--67--

Wonderland Trail

Rating:	Easiest
Round trip:	Up to 7.6 miles
Hiking time:	5 hours
Elevation gain:	1,300 feet
High point:	4,100 feet
Best season:	December through early April
Maps:	Green Trails: Mount Rainier West No. 269
Who to contact:	Mount Rainier National Park
	See page189 for map.

Snowshoe through some of the oldest, most beautiful ancient forest left in Washington's Cascades while enjoying views of the rolling, crashing waters of the milky Nisqually River. Families will appreciate the nearly flat, easy trek through the trees along the first half of the route, while those with an appetite for more adventure will enjoy the last half of the hike as it skirts the base of a steep slope, climbs steadily along the rushing river, and passes a pair of pretty waterfalls on its way to Paradise River Camp.

To get there, drive east from Tacoma on State Route 7 and bear right onto State Route 706 at the town of Elbe. Continue east through the Nisqually Entrance of the park, and proceed to Longmire Ranger Station and Lodge. Park in the plowed area behind the lodge.

From the ranger station, hike east along the Wonderland Trail. (Find the trailhead to the left of the ranger station.) The trail is nestled alongside the Road to Paradise for the first half mile, and then is pinched tight between the road and the Nisqually River for a few hundred feet before the road angles left away from the river and trail. The forest around the trail is Douglas fir and cedar. An assortment of wildlife thrives in this rich forest environment, and the most visible member of the forest community is the fearless gray jay, a.k.a. camp-robber jay, a.k.a. whiskey jack. These birds act as if they are all starving as they flit from limb to limb in the trees around the trail whenever hikers are near. The brazen beggars will even go so far as to land on a raised arm, a shoulder, or a head if there is a chance of a quick bit of bread or granola. The chittering, flittering chaps are harmless, and if you can resist their piteous begging, they will leave you alone. But be warned, feed one and all will want a bite.

At three-quarters of a mile, the trail skirts the line between forest and riparian environments, with the Nisqually River just a stone's throw away to the right. The trail stays fairly level alongside the river to the 2-mile mark where it passes the picnic area of Cougar Rock Campground. This is the last time the trail approaches the road because the trail crosses the wide Nisqually on a stout bridge and climbs up the Paradise River Valley while the road sticks to the Nisqually Valley. Paradise River is a smaller, more scenic stream, and the trail sticks close to its banks as it skirts along the base of the steep slope of a narrow gorge for a half mile. There is a danger of snow slides here, so avoid in high or moderate avalanche conditions. The gorge slowly opens up and, at 3.3 miles, passes Carter Falls and, at 3.6 miles, Madcap Falls. Both cascades are pretty plunges of the Paradise and are worthy of a photo and leisurely contemplation. Just above Madcap Falls is Paradise River Camp (a small backcountry campsite). Turn around here for a modest day's outing.

A clump of moss, insulated by a covering of snow, endures a cold winter

--*68*--

Reflection and Louise Lakes

Rating: More difficult
Round trip: 6 miles
Hiking time: 4 hours
Elevation gain: 560 feet
High point: 5,100 feet
Best season: December through early May
Maps: Green Trails: Mount Rainier East No. 270 and Paradise No. 270S
Who to contact: Mount Rainier National Park

This trail stays right along the edge of timber line, making it one of the most spectacular routes for snowshoers (and cross-country skiers) in Mount Rainier National Park. The trail provides a wonderful experience in a winter forest, the chance to visit a frozen alpine lake, and subalpine meadows in which to play and soak up the scenery.

To get there, drive east from Tacoma on State Route 7 and bear right onto State Route 706 at the town of Elbe. Continue east through the Nisqually Entrance of the park, and proceed to the Narada Falls View Area parking lot, which is kept plowed each winter.

From the upper end of the parking area, go right along a plowed driveway, passing a warming hut and restrooms, as well as a long maintenance shed, to find the trail. If the snow is stable and not too deep, climb the steep, open slope directly ahead to reach the main trail. If conditions are icy, or the climb looks too steep, follow the orange blazes to the left through the trees as the trail parallels the bottom of the hill. Soon you'll begin angling uphill and will quickly top out on a wide, level trail—it is actually the Paradise-Stevens Canyon Road. Turn right, and snowshoe along this road as it loops out around the flank of Inspiration Point. The road quickly bears to the left and enters a long corridor in the forest. The way has little elevation gain, but it can't be called level because the snow rolls through tree wells and snowdrifts.

This trail through the trees brings you right to the edge of Reflection Lakes—although don't count on seeing your reflection because the lake stays frozen over until June. That doesn't mean, however, that the ice is safe. This is an active volcano, and all that geothermal power keeps warm

The view east over Reflection Lake

springs bubbling around and in most of the lakes in the area. That, in turn, keeps the ice on the lake surface thin and dangerous.

Reflection Lakes is reached in just 1.5 miles, with less than 2 miles left to go to Louise Lake, so take some time and expend a little energy exploring this lake basin and enjoying the stunning views of Mount Rainier, as well as the jagged line of peaks in the Tatoosh Range to the south.

From Reflection Lakes, push on east along the road as it curves through a big southern bend and then drops nearly 300 feet in a mile to loop down to the shore of Louise Lake. If the snow is stable, drop off the road just as it enters that big bend and angle down the slope directly to the lakeshore. A camp on the eastern edge of the lake offers great views of a climbing route up Mount Rainier—someone always seems to be making an attempt at the summit. You'll also find that a camp on the east slope above the lake gives you a fantastic surprise in the morning—a stunning sunrise as the towering peak of Mount Rainier starts to glow first and then the sunlight moves slowly down-slope until the entire 14,411-foot peak is brightly lit.

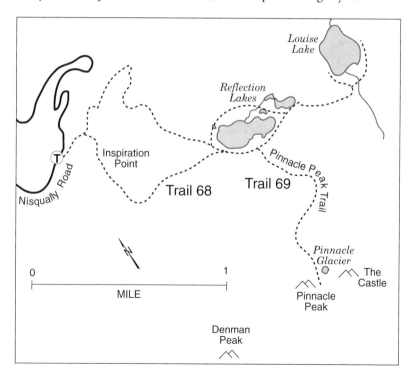

--69--
Pinnacle Saddle

Rating:	Most difficult
Round trip:	6 miles
Hiking time:	5 hours
Elevation gain:	1,400 feet
High point:	6,100 feet
Best season:	December through early May
Maps:	Green Trails: Mount Rainier East No. 270
Who to contact:	Mount Rainier National Park
	See page 198 for map.

Imagine a view that encompasses the three great volcanoes of southern Washington, with Oregon's Mount Hood and Mount Jefferson tossed in for good measure, and the jagged line of the Goat Rocks Peaks capping off the panoramic splendor. That's exactly what's found at the end of this scenic, if somewhat strenuous, trek up the flank of the Tatoosh Range to a wide saddle between Pinnacle Peak and The Castle.

To get there, drive east from Tacoma on State Route 7 and bear right onto State Route 706 at the town of Elbe. Continue east through the Nisqually Entrance of the park, and proceed to the Narada Falls View Area parking lot, which is kept plowed each winter.

Proceed up the trail to Reflection Lakes, and from the southern shore of the larger lake, start a slow, steady climb up the steep meadows to the south. The route heads up a wide, open bowl near the lake's eastern end, providing the most gradual ascent and the least danger of avalanche. Near the top of the snowy meadow, the trail bears right near the tree line and traverses out around a small ridge crest. The snowshoe route lies roughly along the path of the Pinnacle Peak Trail. At the end of the small ridge, bear left with the trail and climb along the crest of the ridge as it angles due south toward Pinnacle Peak. The ridge is thinning forest, so the snowshoeing is easy. Pick the path of least resistance through the pretty snow-laden trees, and keep climbing the moderately sloped ridge crest. Just a mile past Reflection Lakes, the route steepens significantly. To avoid the steep climb, angle left into an open snow field. Although still pitched at an angle, this bowl is less steep than the route straight up Pinnacle

Peak. Follow the open snow field up to a high saddle with Pinnacle Peak on the right and The Castle to the left.

Fanatic peak-baggers may be tempted to try to scramble to the summit of one or the other. But before succumbing to that temptation, bear in mind that well-honed winter climbing skills, and the necessary hardware, are required to make either summit (and the narrow summits are typically crowned with dangerous cornices). The views from this saddle are comparable to what's found at the top of either peak, anyway.

Speaking of views, as soon as you reach the saddle, turn around and soak in the awesome sight of Mount Rainier looming to the north. The saddle looks out across the valley to easily seen Paradise and, higher on the mountain, Camp Muir. Walk to the southern edge of the saddle, and look out across the Gifford Pinchot National Forest to Mount Adams, the Goat Rocks, Mount St. Helens, Mount Hood, and on really clear days, Mount Jefferson on the far southern horizon.

At the ridge crest, Pinnacle Saddle

--7O--
Mazama Ridge

Rating: More difficult
Round trip: 6 miles
Hiking time: 5 hours
Elevation gain: 900 feet
High point: 5,700 feet
Best season: December through early April
Maps: Green Trails: Mount Rainier East No. 270 and Paradise No. 270S
Who to contact: Mount Rainier National Park

This is a wonderful trail for snowshoers of all tastes. Like to 'shoe where there are great panoramic vistas of mountain peaks? No problem. Like trails with pretty local scenery? This one has some of the finest subalpine meadows and forests in the country, all blanketed in the deepest snow found in Washington. Want to watch other recreationists play? Snowboarders and telemark skiers love this trail, with its many open slopes on which they can practice their turns. Looking for a chance to see wild-life? In addition to the wide variety of avian life—from camp-robber and Stellar's jays to ravens and red-tailed hawks—snowshoe hares, red foxes, and a variety of small, scurrying beasts inhabit the forest fringes.

Snowshoers will also find they are not bound by a specific trail on this route. Hiking up Mazama Ridge, they can amble off in any direction and pick their own paths through the deep snow of the meadows along the ridge crest. There is no finer place for snowshoers to enjoy the total freedom of movement that their 'shoes afford them.

To get there, drive east from Tacoma on State Route 7 and bear right onto State Route 706 at the town of Elbe. Continue east through the Nisqually Entrance of the park, and proceed up the plowed road to the Paradise Lodge Parking Area.

Climb the slope above the parking area and head off to the right, staying above Paradise Lodge, to enter the broad open meadows of the upper Paradise Valley. Staying above the roadway, cross Edith Creek on a wide footbridge, just above the ice-cloaked waterfalls. From the bridge, head due east, traversing around the head of the Paradise Valley, to ap-proach the steep wall of Mazama Ridge at about 0.7 mile.

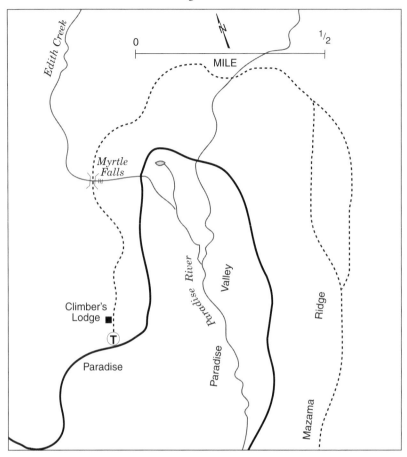

Start up the ridge, angling right (south) while climbing steeply for a half mile to attain the ridge crest at 5,700 feet. Cross to the eastern side of the ridge crest for great views in that direction. Then turn right and follow the ridge south through thin stands of dwarf trees (their growth stunted by the howling winds that frequently scour this open ridge) and wide open meadows. Looking south, the multiple peaks of the Tatoosh Range—Pinnacle Peak, The Castle, Unicorn, Boundary Peak, and the rest—are visible as a jagged line against the sky. At the southern end of the Mazama Ridge, near the 2.5-mile mark, look down onto Reflection and Louise Lakes and east along the deep cut of Stevens Canyon. To the north, Mount Rainier towers over it all.

To return, go north along the western edge of the ridge to the tracks left on the climb up. Turn and follow those tracks back to Paradise.

Incredibly heavy rime ice coats trees on Mazama Ridge

--71--

Panorama Point

Rating:	Most difficult
Round trip:	5 miles
Hiking time:	4 hours
Elevation gain:	1,300 feet
High point:	6,800 feet
Best season:	December through early May
Maps:	Green Trails: Mount Rainier East No. 270 and Paradise No. 270S
Who to contact:	Mount Rainier National Park

The open snowfields, bowls, and meadows above Paradise draw snow-lovers of all kinds, from skiers to snowboarders, but snowshoers have the edge on them all on the way up. Climbing the sometimes steep slopes is best done on a stout pair of snowshoes, and while the skiers and boarders

Looking up the treeless slopes above Panorama Point

may zip down faster than snowshoers, they blast past the awesome views that snowshoers can admire at leisure as they slowly descend the mountain's flank. Countless opportunities for snowshoeing can be found in the open area, but heading up toward Panorama Point is the best of the bunch.

To get there, drive east from Tacoma on State Route 7 and bear right onto State Route 706 at the town of Elbe. Continue east through the Nisqually Entrance of the park, and proceed up the plowed road to the Paradise Lodge Parking Area.

Snowshoe up the steep meadow behind the Climber's Lodge, skirt around the left side of the groomed-snow play area, and hike north along the west side of the tree-covered crown of Alta Vista peak. The route rolls uphill through meadows and thin tree cover, with excellent views of the mountain when the weather is clear.

From the small saddle on the north side of Alta Vista, climb along the prominent ridge crest as it leads straight toward Mount Rainier. The route parallels the massive finger of Nisqually Glacier, and at 1.5 miles, crosses a flat bench aptly named Glacier Vista. This is the best place to find a panoramic view of the sprawling glacier as it stretches from high on the flank of the mountain nearly to the Road to Paradise. If you are tired from the relentless climbing, turn back here knowing you've experienced some of the best views of the route; or catch your breath while

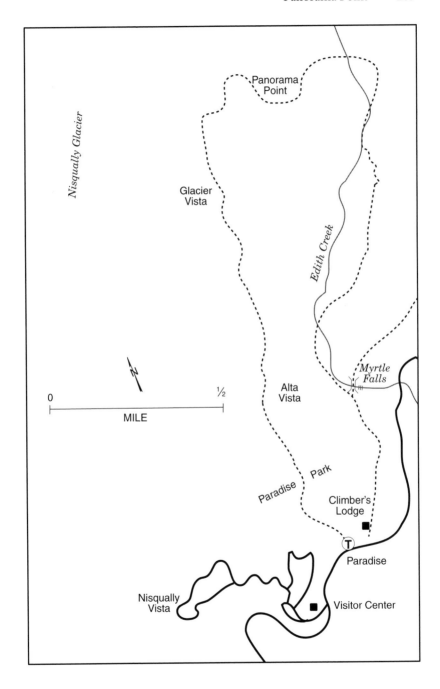

Panorama
Point

Nisqually Glacier

Glacier
Vista

Edith Creek

N

0   ½

MILE

Alta
Vista

Myrtle
Falls

Paradise   Park

Climber's
Lodge

T

Paradise

Nisqually
Vista

Visitor Center

soaking in the scenery, and then continue up to Panorama Point.

From Glacier Vista, the route climbs steeply northeast through open hillside meadows (with a few thin stands of wind-savaged alpine trees) to another broad bench nearly a mile farther up the mountain. (The distance varies from 0.6 to 1 mile, depending on how steeply you climb.)

Panorama Point lives up to its name, with grand views of the mighty mountain, its lower flanks, and the serrated ridge line of the Tatoosh Range to the south. On clear, cold days, the rocky spires of the Goat Rocks Wilderness Area as well as the perfect cone of Mount Adams are visible to the southeast.

To return to Paradise, head east across the bench of Panorama Point and descend the wide open slopes of the upper Edith Creek Basin. The basin is wide and you can pick your own path once you enter it, but use caution when making the first drop into the basin. For the safest route, hike southeast no less than a half mile from Panorama Point to skirt out and around the steepest slopes, which are always heavily corniced. Once past the obvious cornices and steep drops, head down the slope along Edith Creek and follow it all the way down to Paradise, passing under Alta Vista and entering the upper Paradise Valley to approach the Paradise Lodge and Visitor Center from the east.

--72--
Silver Falls/Grove of the Patriarchs

Rating:	More difficult
Round trip:	3 miles/5 miles
Hiking time:	2 hours/3.5 hours
Elevation gain:	200 feet/400 feet
High point:	2,500 feet
Best season:	January through early March
Maps:	Green Trails: Mount Rainier East No. 270
Who to contact:	Mount Rainier National Park

This is an excellent route for snowshoers looking for a quiet forest outing, without the need to struggle with a lot of climbing and routefinding. The trail is generally flat and wide, and it is low enough so that the snow doesn't get so deep that the trail is ill-defined. The trail is so easy to follow that snowshoers can spend their time enjoying the views around them rather

Snow-lined creek near the Grove of the Patriarchs, Silver Falls route

than looking for the path through the trees. The route follows the gorgeous Ohanapecosh River upstream from Ohanapecosh Campground, slicing through lush old forests and passing the beautiful Silver Falls—made even more beautiful by the silver shards of ice that line the rocks around the cascade. The trail continues up the valley to a haunting stand of massive trees on a broad island in the middle of the Ohanapecosh River.

The Grove of the Patriarchs is a beautiful cathedral in summer months, but when the forest floor is blanketed with a white quilt of snow, the enormous trees of the grove are made to seem even larger than they are. The stark contrast of the brilliant white snow and the dark, scaly tree trunks makes the immensity of the cedars, hemlocks, and firs almost incomprehensible.

To get there, from Packwood drive east on US 12 to its junction with State Route 123 and turn left (north). Drive to the Ohanapecosh Campground on the left. (At times, this is the end of the plowed road, although usually the road is plowed another 1.5 miles to the Stevens Canyon Entrance.) Park in the plowed lot at the campground.

Snowshoe down the road leading into the campground, and just before the road crosses the Ohanapecosh River, turn into the northern loop of campsites. The trail begins at the northernmost end of this loop, just before it turns east away from the river.

Start up the trail as it climbs gradually to a bench above the river and rolls north through thin forests between the river and the road. The trail is wide and offers plenty of views of the river while staying well clear of the roadway (which is frequently used by skiers and occasionally by snow-mobilers). This trail is generally unused except by other snowshoers, so there is plenty of solitude and quiet time along the way.

The trail crosses the river at 1.5 miles on a wide, rustic bridge with pretty views up the river to the crashing waters of Silver Falls. The bridge is usually slick, but with handrails on both sides, the crossing is easy and the wide deck is spacious enough for you to pause and enjoy the views.

For a closer look at the falls, continue across the bridge and turn right on the trail on the far bank to climb upstream alongside the falls. After snapping a few pictures and admiring the cascade, either turn back and return to Ohanapecosh Campground or continue upstream for another half mile (stay right at the junction a few hundred yards above the falls) to the Stevens Canyon Road. Cross the wide road near the tollbooths, and head up the wide, well-signed trail to the Grove of the Patriarchs. The trail skirts along the west bank of the river and, in a half mile (mile 2.5), crosses the river on a narrow suspension bridge. This bridge is usually very slick, so cross with extreme care, making full use of both handrails, and enter the cathedral-like stand of ancient trees that is the Grove of the Patriarchs.

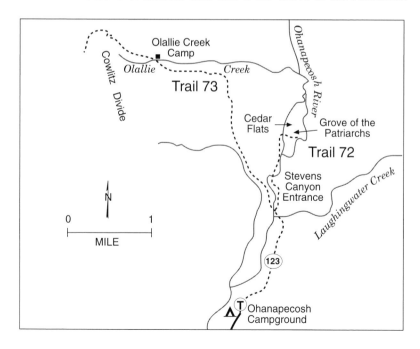

After enjoying the scenic splendor of the forest, return the way you came, or follow the Stevens Canyon Road south to Ohanapecosh Campground for a quicker return.

--73--
Olallie Creek

Rating:	Most difficult
Round trip:	6.8 miles
Hiking time:	7 hours
Elevation gain:	1,800 feet
High point:	3,800 feet
Best season:	January through early March
Maps:	Green Trails: Mount Rainier East No. 270
Who to contact:	Mount Rainier National Park
	See page 208 for map.

Often overlooked, this trail is overflowing with opportunities for snowshoers looking for solitude along a quiet forest path. The huge, old trees, abundant wildlife, and remarkable sylvan environment of this area, coupled with a general dearth of winter visitors, means this trail is an ideal retreat from the busy schedules of modern life. There are no sweeping panoramas, no drop-dead gorgeous views of peaks, valleys, or rivers. But there are endless small graces along the route—snow-draped ferns, ice-adorned lichens, cathedral-like stands of cedar and fir, tracks of birds and animals to identify, and usually plenty of the birds and animals who laid the tracks to see and enjoy.

The trail can be enjoyed as a simple, unhurried day hike or as a multiday snowshoe trek, with multiple options for an ultimate destination, including a high ridge route that does offer incredible views and picturesque panoramas. But the real beauty of this trail is the quiet forest, and that can be enjoyed by hiking as little as the first mile of the route.

To get there, from Packwood drive east on US 12 to its junction with State Route 123 and turn left (north). Drive to the end of the plowed road at the junction with the Stevens Canyon Entrance to Mount Rainier National Park. Occasionally, the road is plowed only as far as the Ohanapecosh Campground. If that is the case, park in the lot at the campground and snowshoe the 1.5 miles to Stevens Canyon along the roadway.

Along the Olallie Creek route

Just west of the tollbooths at the Stevens Canyon Entrance, turn left and enter the forest on a wide trail, signed Silver Falls Trail, and hike southwest a quarter mile to a junction with a trail on the right. Turn right onto this path, signed Olallie Creek, and hike through the forest a few hundred yards, cross the wide Stevens Canyon Road, and reenter the forest on the north side of the highway. The trail climbs steadily but not too steeply for the next 2.5 miles, traversing a lush old-growth forest as it ascends the slopes. At 1.7 miles, the trail crosses a small creek and, at 2 miles, climbs a short series of switchbacks before turning west and traversing the slope above Olallie Creek.

The trail levels out near mile 3 and tapers toward the creek in the valley bottom. Near mile 3.4, the trail crosses the stream at Olallie Creek Camp. Enjoy a quiet lunch in this serene forest camp, and then retrace your steps. If you are looking for more adventure, continue up the trail as it ascends Olallie Creek Valley and ends at a junction with the Wonderland Trail at the crest of the Cowlitz Divide. Head north on the Wonderland, and climb a steep ridge to Indian Bar Camp (9.7 miles from the trailhead) with its stunning views of the mountain and all the peaks to the south.

--74--

Packwood Lake

Rating:	Most difficult
Round trip:	9 miles
Hiking time:	7 hours
Elevation gain:	500 feet
High point:	3,200 feet
Best season:	Late January through early March
Maps:	Green Trails: Packwood No. 302
Who to contact:	Gifford Pinchot National Forest, Cowlitz Valley Ranger District, Packwood Office

This lake is a popular summer destination for family campers, and it is even more impressive when visited in winter. The large lake is just outside the border of the Goat Rocks Wilderness Area, and an old service road slices through the forest alongside a water pipeline all the way to the dam at the lower end of the lake. This road provides easy early-winter access to skiers and snowmobilers. After a few snowstorms, the road is made impassable by avalanches, and snowshoers will find the trail through the young forest silent and seemingly made with them in mind. The trail, though, is in avalanche country, too, so snowshoers must know the current avalanche conditions and should avoid this trail when the danger is any higher than moderate.

The hike from the road end to the lake weaves through thick, old forest, and views are limited. But the local scenery makes up for the lack of distant sights.

To get there, from Seattle drive south on Interstate 5 to US 12. Continue east on US 12 to Packwood. Turn right at the Packwood Ranger Station, and continue 6 miles on the Packwood Lake Road to the trailhead.

Whether you walk or drive to the official trailhead, you'll want to spend a few minutes there. The view is remarkable because a big, open window in the trees perfectly frames that big snowcone to the north, Mount Rainier.

Upon leaving the trailhead, the trail is fairly wide and easy to follow. It dips immediately into the sparse old forest and enters a shadowy world of green, gray, and white. The trail meanders up and down, gradually gaining elevation over the first 4 miles only to drop more than 200 feet in the last half mile before rolling out along the lakeshore. In periods of unusually heavy snow, the 4 miles of trail may be stretched by an additional 2 or 3 miles of road walking. But that extra mileage just makes for a more rewarding payoff at camp at day's end.

The snow underfoot is bright against the dull gray fir and cedar tree trunks, while overhead, waxy green boughs and droopy beards of green lichen provide color to this cold sylvan world. But the best of the scenery is not the stationary stuff around you; it's the small gray streaks that flit from tree to tree. These feathery bundles of energy go by many names—whiskey jacks, gray jays, or camp-robbers—but regardless of what you call them, you will enjoy their company.

The south shore of the lake is the safest haven for camp because it is gently graded and well forested, which minimizes the threat of snowslides. It also offers the best views. Plenty of sheltered areas for camps are scattered along the length of the lake, but smart campers will pitch their tents at the far end of the lake so they can enjoy the fiery sunsets that illuminate Mount Rainier to the north. If weather clouds the horizon, though, the views to the south are nearly as stunning—the 7,487-foot Johnson Peak looms large at the head of the Packwood Creek Valley.

A word of warning: amidst all this beauty, danger lurks close by. The snowy mantle covering the lake looks stable and strong, but this is a big body of water at the relatively low elevation of 2,900 feet, so the ice is almost always too thin to bear the weight of heavy bodies tramping across it. Stay off the lake. If you don't, you'll likely end up in the lake, and in winter that means hypothermia.

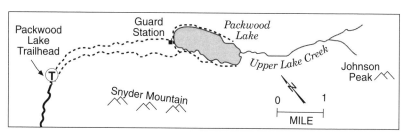

-- 75 --
Sand Lake

Rating: Most difficult
Round trip: 9 miles
Hiking time: 7 hours
Elevation gain: 900 feet
High point: 5,300 feet
Best season: Late December through early March
Maps: Green Trails: White Pass No. 303
Who to contact: Gifford Pinchot National Forest, Cowlitz Valley Ranger District, Packwood Office

Skirting beautiful high alpine meadows, the Pacific Crest Trail rolls north from White Pass on a gentle climb, providing snowshoers with a wonderful opportunity to enjoy the high country of the Cascades in winter without a long slog up a wide logging road. This trail dips into thick old stands of forest, but it is the open meadows, long ridges, and high peaks that make this a special trail. Pass by large circular plains of snow (frozen lakes) and rolling dunes of drifted snow. This trail offers an immersion into the dreamlands of mountain country in winter.

Snowshoers of all abilities will find enjoyment here as the terrain is open and gentle. They can hike as much, or as little, as they desire.

To get there, from Packwood drive east on US 12 to the summit of White Pass. Park on the north (left) side of the highway in the large overnight parking area near the White Pass Nordic Center (just west of the large hotel).

The Pacific Crest Trail actually crosses US 12 to the east of the ski area, but you can catch it by skirting Leech Lake—which abuts the parking area—on its south shore, staying well to the side of the groomed ski tracks, for a half mile. Follow the curve of the lakeshore to the north, and just like that, jump on the Pacific Crest Trail. The trail climbs gently through a thick stand of fir and then open meadow for 1.4 miles to a small creek basin. Stay left here (a trail also leads off to the right, cruising down the creek valley through open forest to Dog Lake in 1.5 mile), and traverse a large meadow at the head of the creek valley, passing the nearly round Deer Lake Basin at 2.7 miles. At the lake, the trail turns north once more and rolls gently uphill through meadows broken occasionally by thin stands of wind-gnarled trees. The trail is obliterated by snow in this open country, but the

Mount Adams from the Sand Lake route

route stays along the broad crest of a shallow ridge as it leads due north.

At 3.3 miles, find Sand Lake on the right (east) side of the ridge. The lake is often obscured because the gentle slope of the banks and the surrounding open country allow the snow to drift in and cover it. So look for an oblong flat surface just below the ridge line at 5,300 feet. This is the place to turn around, except if you plan on pitching camp out in the winter wilderness. Then hike on up the trail as it rolls north, pushing through more meadows, forests, and past small alpine lakes.

The Sand Lake Basin and the small ridge above it offer nice views of the surrounding peaks, including Cramer Mountain to the north, Spiral Butte to the east, and Round Mountain to the southeast. It's sometimes possible to see the summit of Mount Adams protruding on the southern horizon, too.

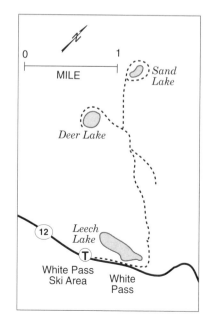

--76--
Cramer Lake

Rating:	Most difficult
Round trip:	9 miles
Hiking time:	7 hours
Elevation gain:	800 feet
High point:	5,000 feet
Best season:	Late December through early March
Maps:	Green Trails: White Pass No. 303
Who to contact:	Gifford Pinchot National Forest, Cowlitz Valley Ranger District, Packwood Office

This route offers terrain and scenery similar to that found along the Pacific Crest Trail. But far fewer people visit the Cramer Lake Trail, so snowshoers can add solitude to the list of wonders they'll encounter along the route. Starting at the shore of a wide lake basin, this route has views of pretty peaks, meandering creeks—sometimes in old-growth forest settings, sometimes weaving gracefully through open meadows—and long, panoramic views of the south Cascade summits and deep canyons of the eastern foothills.

Although this is a backcountry trail, the route is generally easy to follow with some moderate climbing, so most snowshoers with a solid hiking background will enjoy the workout and the rewards found here.

To get there, from Packwood drive east on US 12 to the summit of White Pass. Continue east 1.5 miles to Dog Lake Campground. Generally a wide pullout is cleared at both the west end of the lake (near Dog Lake Campground) and at the east end, near the highway bridge over the lake's outlet stream. Park in whichever is available.

From the highway, snowshoe west along the southern edge of the lake and pick up the trail at the north side of the Dog Lake Campground. The trail traverses the slope away from the lake, staying above the small feeder stream that pours in from the north. A mile up the trail, cross the creek in a thin stand of trees and begin a moderately steep climb northeast along the slope.

The forest gives way frequently to large, open meadows, and the round top of Spiral Butte dominates the view to the east. At 4,800 feet, about 2 miles out from the trailhead, the trail turns left and heads straight north across open meadows and thin forest. The trail here is fairly flat and straight, leading to the shores of Cramer Lake at 4.5 miles.

For a variation on the return, start back on the same trail, but just a mile south of the lake, veer southeast toward Spiral Butte. Cross a small creek basin, and traverse the flank of the butte at about 4,900 feet. A long line of open meadows, separated by thin strands of forest, cover the side of the mountain, and you can work your way down to the 4,300-foot level as you continue south around the mountain.

When the Dog Lake Basin is in view, drop down into the thin forest at the north end of the lake and cross the flat meadow to get back to the western side of the lake for the final quarter-mile snowshoe back to the trailhead. Avoid the eastern shore of the lake unless snow conditions are very stable because the lake butts up against a steep avalanche chute.

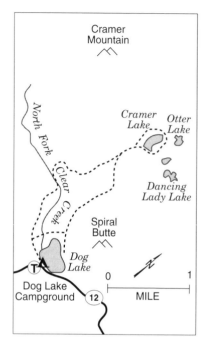

On the way to Cramer Lake

--77--

Goat Peak

Rating: Backcountry
Round trip: 5.6 miles
Hiking time: 5 hours
Elevation gain: 2,600 feet
High point: 5,900 feet
Best season: Late December through early March
Maps: Green Trails: Bumping Lake No. 271
Who to contact: Wenatchee National Forest, Naches Ranger District

This is a winter scramble up a ruthlessly steep trail, but the views and the scenery along the way are unmatched. The route climbs quickly up a steep ridge line on a narrow hiking trail, and snowshoers won't find much to look for in the first mile as they struggle up the slope. Although the trail may be demanding, it is a route used only by snowshoers. So many of the other trails in this area are dominated by cross-country skiers and snowmobilers that snowshoers will welcome the workout knowing that they don't have to share the trail with noisy speedsters.

Snowshoers who enjoy wildlife may want to stroll around the meadows in the valley bottom near the Sno-Park before starting up the trail. A large herd of elk roams this valley, and there is always the possibility that they will be browsing near the Hells Crossing area, so give a look for them before starting the climb.

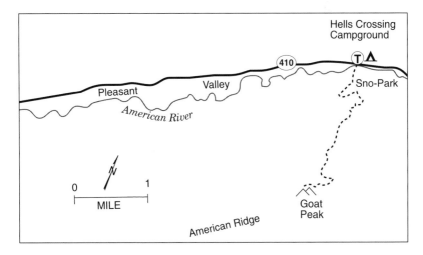

View over the Cascade foothills, Goat Peak route

To get there, from Yakima drive west on US 12 to its junction with State Route 410. Turn right (northwest) onto State Route 410 and drive 34 miles to the Hells Crossing Sno-Park on the left (south), just opposite the Hells Crossing Campground (closed).

The trail climbs south from the Sno-Park, heading up the east side of a small draw. The route isn't too steep for the first half mile, and after that, it makes a long traverse east around the flank of the hill to the ridge crest. At 1 mile, the trail turns vertical as it ascends the steep ridge crest, heading south toward the towering summit of Goat Peak. The route is exposed at times, and there are some tricky pitches, especially near 1.2 miles and again at 1.8 to 2 miles. Treeless sections are occasionally scoured by wind.

The trail dips down onto the eastern side of the ridge at 2.5 miles, and the last quarter mile is a gentle traverse to the top of American Ridge just east of the Goat Peak summit. It is possible to climb to the top of the peak, but the approach on the American Ridge Trail is exposed and heavily corniced at times. It is better to just enjoy the stunning views from the ridge crest at the top of the trail and leave the summitting for a summertime outing.

From the top of American Ridge, the views are outstanding. To the east is the long, open country of the eastern foothills of the Cascades. To the north is Fifes Ridge and 6,375-foot Fife Peak. To the south is the expansive William O. Douglas Wilderness and, beyond, the perfect cone of Mount Adams.

--78--
Mount St. Helens Summit

Rating: Backcountry
Round trip: 8 miles
Hiking time: 9 hours
Elevation gain: 5,700 feet
High point: 8,365 feet
Best season: Late December through early February
Maps: Green Trails: Mount St. Helens Northwest No. 364S
Who to contact: Mount St. Helens National Volcanic Monument

On this climb up Mount St. Helens, snowshoers can simply walk straight up the deep snow piled on the flank of the big volcano, taking a direct approach to the rim of the massive crater. Along the way, they can enjoy sweeping views out over the southern reaches of Washington's Cascades.

Once at the summit, snowshoers can peer cautiously over the edge of the crater rim to see the steaming lava dome building the crater and look out over the miles of destruction wrought by the May 18, 1980, blast. Snowshoers have an advantage over summer climbers in that permits are not needed for midwinter ascents. From May 15 to October 31 every year, anyone attempting the summit must have one of the limited number of climbing permits (only 40 are issued each day). But after the first of November, the mountain is open to anyone who wants to climb its snow-blanketed slopes.

To get there, from Woodland

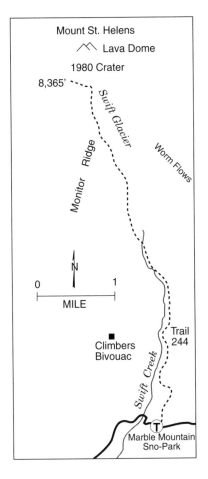

Snowshoers preparing to go above timber line

drive east on State Route 503 to the community of Cougar and continue east another 7 miles to a junction with Forest Service Road No. 83. Turn left (north) onto Road No. 83, and drive 5.8 miles to the Marble Mountain Sno-Park at the end of the plowed road.

From the Sno-Park, snowshoe north on Swift Creek Trail No. 244 as it follows the east bank of the creek toward the mountain. The trail climbs gradually, allowing you to loosen up and get into a good swing for the long, steady climb ahead.

At 2.2 miles, the trail passes a well-marked side trail on the right leading down to June Lake. Stay left and climb northwest, moving above timber line to cross Swift Creek at 2.5 miles. Once past Swift Creek, continue to traverse to the left (northwest) for another quarter mile, and then turn straight up the slope and start the long slog to the top. The idea is to follow the path of least resistance, flowing with the contours of the mountain. If the slope becomes too steep directly above, contour to the left or right until the pitch of the slope lessens somewhat or a more attractive avenue of ascent is found. By maintaining a bearing of nearly due north, with just a bit of correction to the west, you can top out on the ridge near the upper end of Monitor Ridge—the long, high spine to the west of Swift Creek. Monitor Ridge is the route used by summer climbers and leads to the best viewing site on the crater rim, although the true summit is found around to the northwest from the top of Monitor Ridge.

Because the upper slopes of Mount St. Helens are open and treeless, a great deal of wind scours the snowpack up there. This can result in deep drifts of soft snow or sheets of hard-packed snow and ice, depending on the conditions during the storms. Come prepared with snowshoes featuring aggressive mountaineering cleats on both heel and toe and carry—and know how to use—an ice ax for self-arresting in the event of a fall. This is a mountain climb and winter mountaineering skills are required.

--79--

June Lake

Rating:	Backcountry
Round trip:	4.5 miles
Hiking time:	3 hours
Elevation gain:	500 feet
High point:	3,100 feet
Best season:	Late December through early March
Maps:	Green Trails: Mount St. Helens Northwest No. 364S
Who to contact:	Mount St. Helens National Volcanic Monument
	See page 225 for map.

The June Lake Trail is a beautiful hike any time of year, but exploring the trail on snowshoes, with the deep old forest, wide lake basin, and crashing waterfall all swaddled in a blanket of white, is the only way to enjoy the truly wild nature of the area. The trail is a gentle path through the woods, and snowshoers of all ages and abilities will appreciate and enjoy the remarkable beauty of the route.

Located on the south side of the big volcano, this trail doesn't delve into the blast zone, nor does the scenery make snowshoers think about the volcanic nature of the area. Indeed, if the eruption of 1980 comes to mind, it's usually in the context of "I can't believe an area this beautiful survived such a big eruption." Mount St. Helens' summit is visible along the trail to the lake, but looking up at the south flank of the mountain, with its snowy mantle of winter, it looks like just another big, beautiful peak. And June Lake is such a remarkably beautiful setting that it doesn't need the powerful imagery of the eruption to make it a wonderful snowshoeing destination.

To get there, from Woodland drive east on State Route 503 to the community of Cougar and continue east another 7 miles to a junction with Forest Service Road No. 83. Turn left (north) onto Road No. 83, and drive 5.8 miles to the Marble Mountain Sno-Park at the end of the plowed road. Small maps of the local winter trails are generally available in the kiosk inside the warming hut at the Sno-Park.

From the Sno-Park, snowshoe north from the upper parking lot on the well-signed Pine Martin Trail No. 245E. This trail, which is often groomed for skiers, parallels the road, but it is off limits to snowmobiles. (You can also hike up the road to the June Lake Trailhead, but it is often crowded with speeding snowmobiles.) The trail heads north for three-quarters of a mile, and then hooks right (east) and dips down to join the road at 1 mile. After using the road bridge to cross the wide Lake Creek, turn left and snowshoe into the large parking area of the well-marked June Lake Trailhead. The trail leaves the north end of the broad lot and crosses a large meadow in full view

Along the trail to June Lake

of Mount St. Helens. The open, treeless slopes are painted stark white by the drifting snow, and most weekends when the weather is clear, snowshoers on the June Lake Trail can watch snowshoers and skiers climbing the Monitor Ridge route (see trip 78) to the summit of the volcano.

The trail stays well above Lake Creek as it climbs gradually through a few stands of second-growth forest and open clearcuts before finally crossing into the protected National Monument at 2.4 miles. The last few hundred yards of trail dip steeply down to cross the creek on a wide bridge before rolling north to the shore of June Lake. Across the lake, on the right, is a waterfall cascading down through a curtain of interlaced icicles. The wide bench at the lakeshore makes a wonderful picnic spot with its spectacular views.

--*80*--
Worm Flows

Rating:	Backcountry
Round trip:	7 miles
Hiking time:	4.5 hours
Elevation gain:	500 feet
High point:	3,100 feet
Best season:	Late December through early March
Maps:	Green Trails: Mount St. Helens Northwest No. 364S
Who to contact:	Mount St. Helens National Volcanic Monument

The Worm Flows, long rippling lava flows from an eruption eons ago, roll down the southeast flank of Mount St. Helens creating a remarkably unique environment. The flows are somewhat masked by winter's heavy blanket of snow, but the undulating landscape testifies to their existence. The lava flowed and solidified into a roll, and then more lava flowed out over it, only to solidify into another roll. And on, and on, and on. The winter trails here barely touch on the Worm Flows, but they do offer great views of this geologic oddity on the flank of the mountain.

This route also offers an easy snowshoe trek through a chain of open meadows, linked by stands of pretty forest. There are opportunities to look up at the stark south face of Mount St. Helens or just enjoy the more immediate surroundings of sun-dappled meadows, sparkling woodland streams, and snow-laden evergreens. Look for a variety of birds here, from Stellar's and gray jays to ptarmigan and grouse, as well as small mammals burrowing through, and skittering over, the snow. Martens, weasels (with their winter white coats), coyotes, and raccoons may be seen here—or at least the tracks they leave behind.

To get there, from Woodland drive east on State Route 503 to the community of Cougar and continue east another 7 miles to a junction with Forest Service Road No. 83. Turn left (north) onto Road No. 83, and drive 5.8 miles to the Marble Mountain Sno-Park at the end of the plowed road. Small maps of the local winter trails are generally available in the kiosk inside the warming hut at the Sno-Park.

Snowshoe north from the upper parking lot on the well-signed, nonmotorized Pine Martin Trail No. 245E, which parallels the road (open to snowmobilers) for a mile. The road and trail merge briefly at 1 mile so that snowshoers and skiers can safely cross the frigid waters of Lake Creek. Then the trail climbs to the left and away from the road once more, crosses the trail to June Lake, and heads east to its end at mile 1.8. Although the Pine Marten Trail ends here, several other trails begin. A large kiosk/message board is posted here each winter, with a map of the local trails well marked on it.

On the slope below the Worm Flows

Several routes are possible, but the one most appropriate for snow-shoers is the Middle Sasquatch Trail across the base of the Worm Flows. This trail, No. 236A, is a 3.4-mile loop through meadows, forests, and Worm Flows. From the end of the Pine Marten Trail and the trail kiosk, go left and snowshoe up a gentle hill between two creek basins. Well-placed blazes on trees and poles mark the route, but if they aren't visible, just stay on a northerly bearing, climbing along an old, faint logging road. (It is some-times difficult to see the road when the snow is deep or heavily drifted.) At the top of the ridge, near mile 2.7, find a well-marked trail intersection with a very distinct logging road heading east. A less-prominent trail leads straight ahead through the junction. This is the start of the longer loop option, which adds about 2 miles to the total trip distance. For the Middle Trail, though, go right onto the logging road and follow it on a long, gradual drop through open forest for a mile to another well-marked trail junction. To the left is the end of the longer loop option, so go right to complete the Middle Trail loop. The trail curves south for a quarter mile, and then turns abruptly west and completes the loop portion of the hike at 4.2 miles. Follow the Pine Marten Trail back to the Sno-Park from the end of the loop.

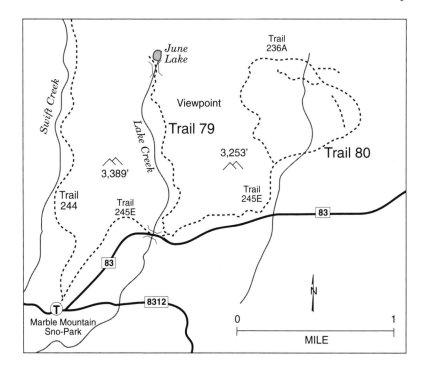

-- *81* --

Table Rock/Squaw Peak

Rating: Most difficult/Backcountry
Round trip: 22 miles
Hiking time: 2 to 3 days
Elevation gain: 1,800 feet
High point: 5,900 feet
Best season: December through February
Maps: USGS: Godman Springs, Deadman Peak
Who to contact: Umatilla National Forest, Pomeroy Ranger District

This hike starts out easy and gets progressively more difficult to the end—at which point the views make the whole effort worthwhile. Table Rock is a flat-topped ridge crest that is home to an old, still-used fire-lookout tower. Due west of the lookout is the untouched Mill Creek Watershed, a deep forested basin that has been protected and placed off-limits to all—this watershed provides the drinking water for the Walla Walla area.

The lookout is accessible by four-wheel drive vehicles in the summer, but shortly after the first snows fall in autumn, the road is closed by slides and avalanches. Winter hikers, in fact, have to avoid sections of the road and hike the knife-edged ridges for the last couple of miles.

To get there, from Dayton turn south off US 12 onto Fourth Street (North Touchet Road) and drive south 19.5 miles to the Touchet Corrals Sno-Park. The parking area is on the left.

The parking area was built by volunteer labor from the local snowmobile club back in the late 1970s when the nearby Bluewood downhill-ski resort was built. Snowmobilers continue to be the primary users of this Sno-Park, but snowshoers and skiers also flock to the area. Most trails begin at the end of a long "expressway" that parallels the road for nearly a mile before ducking under the road, through a 6-foot-tall culvert. On the other side, the trail climbs a steep bank and follows the snow-covered road. Just a couple of miles up the road, the trail forks at a registration box. Stop here long enough to sign in, and then continue straight ahead on the main road. In just a half mile, another fork is met. Stay right at this junction, and continue to climb for another mile and a half as more and more views greet your eyes. The road you are following was cut into a steep valley wall, but in twenty years of enjoying this area, I've never seen a single avalanche on this section. As you near the head of this valley, the route levels off in a

Lookout tower on the broad summit of Table Rock

broad open meadow. Most traffic (skiers and snowmobilers) will take off to the left, cutting through the meadow to angle back toward the top of the ski area. Take the path to the southwest into the trees.

After a long, arcing half mile, a third junction is encountered. This is where you leave everyone else behind and head for the wild country. Take a left onto this narrow track into the trees and begin climbing a twisting, turning two-track path. This route parallels the boundary of the Wenaha-Tucannon Wilderness Area. If you step twenty paces or so to the left, you are in the wilderness.

This route climbs gradually, occasionally breaking into small open meadows with views into the deep Wenaha Valley. Take a few minutes to study the valley below because you might see elk, or at least their paths worn into the deep snow. At about 8.5 miles, in a shallow saddle, you leave the road. Hike into the deep snow to your right until you reach the top of a small prominence. Bear south once more, sticking to the contour of the ridge top. The ridge grows ever steeper and more narrow until, after about 2 miles, you find yourself looking down into a deep saddle in the ridge line. The ridge crest is no more than 12 feet wide at this point and at the bottom of the saddle—some 200 feet below. As you start the final half-mile climb to the lookout tower ahead, the ridge narrows to 6 feet in places.

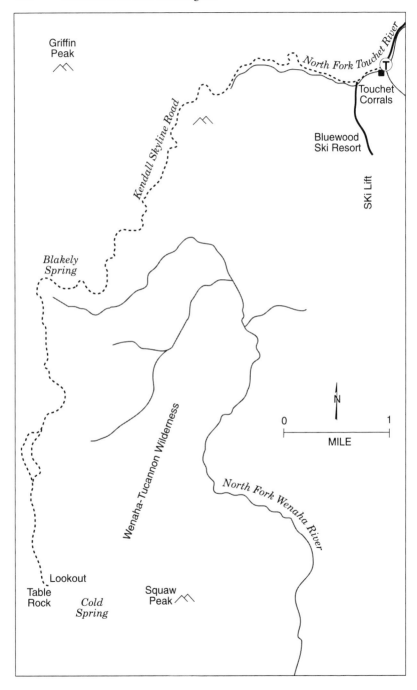

Stick to the middle, and you'll be fine—you're actually walking on rock here. Fierce winds whip up out of the Mill Creek Basin on your right and crash down into the Wenaha Valley on your left.

At the top of the final pitch, find the lookout tower—now boarded up and secured against the bitter winter winds. Enjoy the view, and then move off to the eastern edge of the rocky plateau where an old ranger cabin, stock shed, and corral are found at the edge of the forest. Set up camp on the leeward side of these buildings for a quiet night.

If you have any energy left after making camp, follow the road east, down past the cabin, and in just a quarter mile, you'll encounter the main road (which you abandoned some miles before). Cross this road, and hike to the top of the cone-shaped peak directly ahead. This is Squaw Peak, and it is within the Wenaha-Tucannon Wilderness. It is about the same elevation as Table Rock, but where the view from the lookout is down into the protected Mill Creek Watershed, the view from Squaw Peak is down into the protected wilderness area. Looking south, you'll see the Oregon Blue Mountains (just 2 miles as the crow flies) and on clear days, you can make out the jagged peaks of the Seven Devils bordering Hells Canyon, as well as the peaks of the Wallowa Mountains.

Snowshoers on the shore of Packwood Lake

Appendix

Addresses and Telephone Numbers

Mount Pilchuck State Park
c/o Washington State Parks Northwest Region
220 Walnut Street, Box 487
Burlington, WA 98233
(360) 755-9231

Mount Rainier National Park
Tahoma Woods, Star Route
Ashford, WA 98104
(360) 569-2211

Mount St. Helens National Volcanic Monument
42218 NE Yale Bridge Road
Amboy, WA 98601-9715
(360) 247-3900

Olympic National Park
3002 Mount Angeles Road
Port Angeles, WA 98362
(360) 452-0330

GIFFORD PINCHOT NATIONAL FOREST
Cowlitz Valley Ranger District
10024 US Highway 12
Randle, WA 98377-9105
(360) 497-1100

MOUNT BAKER–SNOQUALMIE NATIONAL FOREST

Darrington Ranger District
1405 Emmens Street
Darrington, WA 98241
(360) 436-1155

Mount Baker Ranger District
2105 Highway 20
Sedro Woolley, WA 98284
(360) 856-5700

North Bend Ranger District
42404 SE North Bend Way
North Bend, WA 98045
(425) 888-1421

Skykomish Ranger District
74920 NE Stevens Pass Highway
Skykomish, WA 98288
(360) 677-2414

White River Ranger District
857 Roosevelt Avenue SE
Enumclaw, WA 98022
(360) 825-6585

OKANOGAN NATIONAL FOREST

Methow Valley Ranger District/Twisp Office
502 Glover
Twisp, WA 98856
(509) 997-2131

Methow Valley Ranger District/Winthrop Office
24 West Chewuch
Winthrop, WA 98862
(509) 997-4000

OLYMPIC NATIONAL FOREST
Quilcene Ranger District
20482 Highway 101
Quilcene, WA 98376
(360) 765-2200

UMATILLA NATIONAL FOREST
Pomeroy Ranger District
Route 1, Box 53-F
Pomeroy, WA 99347
(509) 843-1891

WENATCHEE NATIONAL FOREST
Cle Elum Ranger District
803 West Second Street
Cle Elum, WA 98922
(509) 674-4411

Lake Wenatchee Ranger District
22976 State Highway 207
Leavenworth, WA 98826
(509) 763-3103

Leavenworth Ranger District
600 Sherbourne Street
Leavenworth, WA 98826
(509) 548-6977

Naches Ranger District
10061 Highway 12
Naches, WA 98937
(509) 653-2205

Snowshoer crossing creek near Artist Point

Index

A

Alaska Lake 150
Alpental Ski Area 143
Alpine Lakes Wilderness 128,
    134, 148, 164
Alta Vista 204
Amabilis Mountain 158
American Ridge 218
Artist Point 48
Austin Pass 48

B

Battle Mountain 113
Bear Lake 85
Big Four Ice Caves 93
Big Four Mountain 92
Black Creek 85
Blue Bell Pass 178
Bluewood Ski Area 226
Boardman Lake 81
Bridge Creek Campground 138
Buck Mountain (near Paul
    Mountain) 105
Buck Mountain Lookout 107
Buck Mountain Road 109
Bullion Basin 177
Bullion Creek 178

C

Cabin Creek Sno-Park 156
Canyon Creek 113

Carter Falls 195
Cascade Creek 64
Cashmere Mountain 138
Cedar Creek 104
Cedar Falls 104
Chiwaukum Creek 134
Chutla Peak 190
Circle Peak 67
Coal Creek Valley 95
Coat Pass 40
Coleman Glacier 41
Coles Corner 133
Commonwealth Basin 144
Cooper Lake 169
Cooper River 169
Cougar Rock Campground 195
Cox Creek 32
Cramer Lake 215
Crystal Creek 64, 68
Crystal Lake 68
Crystal Mountain Ski Area 178

D

Darrington 66
Deer Creek Road 88
Dog Lake Campground 215
Duckbill Mountain 113

E

Eagle Creek 113
Eagle Pass 113

Eagle Peak 190
Eagle Point 33
Early Winters Campground 103
Eight-mile River 106
Eight-mile Sno-Park 106
Eight-mile Trail 137
Elbow Lake Trailhead 52
Elderberry Canyon 111

F
Fire Creek 71
Fisher Lake 120
Flat Campground 106
Foss River, East Fork 115
Foss River Road 115, 119
French Cabin Creek 159

G
Gifford Pinchot National Forest, Cowlitz Valley Ranger District 211, 213, 215
Glacier Creek Gorge 41
Glacier Creek Road 43
Glacier Creek Valley 40
Glacier View Wilderness Area 187
Glacier Vista 204
Goat Peak 218
Goat Rocks Wilderness Area 211
Gold Creek Sno-Park 147, 148, 151
Gold Creek Valley 146
Grove of the Patriarchs 207

H
Heather Creek 76
Heather Lake 75
Heliotrope Ridge 42
Hells Crossing Sno-Park 218
Hex Mountain 162, 166
Hoodsport 39
Huntoon Point 49
Hurricane Hill 29

Hurricane Ridge 29, 32
Hurricane Ridge Visitor Center 30, 32, 34

I
Icicle Creek Road 138
Indian Creek 173
Indian Henry's Hunting Ground 190
Inspiration Point 196
Iron Mountain 59

J
Jackman Ridge 58
Jim Hill Mountain 131
Johnson Peak 212
Jolly Mountain 169
June Lake 220, 221

K
Kelcema Lake 88
Kautz Creek 187
Keechelus Lake 148, 150
Keechelus Ridge 155
Kendall Lakes 74
Kendall Peak 146, 148
Kennedy Creek 72
Kennedy Hot Springs 69
Kulshan Creek 44
Kulshan Ridge 49

L
Lake 22, 78
Lake Christine 187
Lake Creek 222
Lake Evan 81
Lake Susan Jane 122
Lake Valhalla 125
Lanham Lake 131
Lanham Creek 131
Leech Lake 213

Libby Creek Road 111
Lichtenburg Mountain 125
Little Wenatchee River 132
Lone Fir Campground 99
Longmire 193
Lookout Creek 43
Lookout Mountain (North
    Cascades) 40
Lookout Mountain (Methow
    Valley) 110
Louise Lake 198
Loup Loup Pass 107
Lower Lena Lake 37

M
Madcap Falls 195
Mallardy Creek 87
Mallardy Ridge 86
Marble Mountain Sno-Park 220,
    222, 224
Mardee Lake 148
Margaret Lake 153
Marten Creek 90
Martin Peak 181
Mazama 100
Mazama Park 53
Mazama Ridge 201
Meadow Mountain 67
Methow River 98, 99, 100
Methow Valley 99, 103
Middle Fork Nooksack River 50
Middle Sasquatch Trail 225
Mill Creek Sno-Park 131
Mill Creek Valley 122
Mill Creek Watershed 226
Monitor Ridge 221
Mount Angeles 31
Mount Baker 44, 48
Mount Baker Highway 41, 43, 45,
    48, 52
Mount Baker Ski Area 48

Mount Baker–Snoqualmie
    National Forest
    Darrington Ranger District 56,
    59, 61, 64, 67, 69, 78, 80, 84, 86,
    87, 90, 92, 94
    Mount Baker Ranger District
    40, 42, 45, 48, 50, 53
    North Bend Ranger District
    139, 141, 144, 146, 148
    Skykomish Ranger District
    115, 117, 120, 123, 128
    White River Ranger District
    174, 177
Mount Beljica 185
Mount Margaret 150
Mount McCausland 125
Mount Pilchuck 73
Mount Pilchuck State Park 73, 75
Mount Rainier National Park 179,
    182, 184, 187, 190, 194, 196,
    199, 201, 203, 206, 209
Mount Sawyer 120
Mount Shuksan 48
Mount St. Helens Nat'l Volcanic
    Monument 219, 221, 223
Mount Tahoma Scenic Ski Trails
    184
Mount Townsend 36
Mountain Loop Highway 62, 66,
    71, 73, 76, 78, 81, 85, 87, 88, 91,
    93, 95
Mowich Lake 179
Mowich Lake Road 182

N
Narada Falls 196, 199
Necklace Valley 117
Nooksack River 45
North Cascades Highway 96
North Fork River Road 173
Northwest Avalanche Center 20

O

Obstruction Point 34
Ohanapecosh Campground 207, 209
Ohanapecosh River 207
Okanogan National Forest, Methow Valley Ranger District
Twisp Office 107, 110, 112
Winthrop Office 96, 99, 103, 104
Olallie Creek 210
Olympic National Forest, Quilcene Ranger District 35, 37
Olympic National Park 29, 31
Owhi Campground 170

P

Pacific Crest Trail 120, 125, 144, 213
Packwood Lake 211
Panorama Point 204
Paradise 201, 204
Paul Mountain 105
Paul Peak 181, 182
Pine Martin Trail 222, 224
Pinnacle Peak 199
Price Creek Westbound Sno-Park 155
Ptarmigan Ridge 49
Pugh Mountain 67
Pumice Creek 71

Q

Quilcene 36
Quilcene River 36

R

Rampart Ridge (Mount Rainier National Park) 193

Rampart Ridge (Snoqualmie Pass) 146
Rat Trap Pass 66
Red Mountain 144
Reflection Lake 196, 199
River Run Trail 99

S

Salmon la Sac Creek 167
Salmon la Sac Picnic Area and Sno-Park 162, 167, 170
Salmon Ridge Sno-Park 45
Sand Lake 214
Sasse Mountain 166
Sasse Ridge 164
Sauk Mountain 56
Sauk Mountain Road 56
Sauk River 58
Sawtooth Wilderness Area 112
Sawyer Pass 120
Schriebers Meadow 54
Schriebers Meadow–Park Butte Trail 54
Schweitzer Creek Road 81, 84
Sedro Woolley 54, 56, 59
Segelsen Ridge 61
Silver Falls 208, 210
Silver Star 98
Skykomish River 128
Skyline Lake 124
Smith Brook Valley 126
Snoqualmie River 143
Snow Lake 141
Source Lake 141
South Finney Creek Sno-Park 63
Spiral Butte 215
Squaw Peak 229
Steeple Rock 33
Stevens Pass 122, 123

Stillaguamish River 95
Straight Creek 64
Sulphur Creek 54
Sun Top 174
Sun Top Sno-Park 176
Surprise Creek 129
Surprise Lake 129
Swift Creek 220

T
Table Rock 226
Talapus Creek 141
Talapus Lake 140
Tatoosh Range 190, 198
Teanaway Valley 172
The Brothers 40
The Castle 199
Thorp Mountain 159
Timothy Meadows 136
Tonga Ridge 118
Touchet Corrals Sno-Park 226
Trail of the Shadows 193
Tumtum Peak 189
Tumwater Campground 135

U
Umatilla National Forest, Pomeroy
   Ranger District 226

V
Valhalla 125
Valley of Silent Men 37
Van Trump Park 193
Verlot Public Service Center 73,
   76, 78, 81, 85, 87, 88, 91, 93, 95

W
War Creek Campground 113
Washington Pass 96

Washington State Sno-Parks 9, 23
Waterhole Camp 33
weather radio 20
Wenaha-Tucannon Wilderness
   Area 227
Wenatchee National Forest
   Cle Elum Ranger District 150,
   153, 156, 159, 161, 164, 167,
   169, 171
   Lake Wenatchee Ranger
   District 134, 137
   Leavenworth Ranger District
   217
   Naches Ranger District 132
Wenatchee Ridge 132
White Chuck River 66, 69
White Pass 213
White River 176
White Salmon Creek 47
William O. Douglas Wilderness
   218
Winthrop 98, 100, 103, 105
Wonderland Trail 193, 194, 211
Worm Flows 223

THE MOUNTAINEERS, founded in 1906, is a nonprofit outdoor activity and conservation club, whose mission is "to explore, study, preserve, and enjoy the natural beauty of the outdoors. . . ." Based in Seattle, Washington, the club is now the third-largest such organization in the United States, with 15,000 members and five branches throughout Washington State.

The Mountaineers sponsors both classes and year-round outdoor activities in the Pacific Northwest, which include hiking, mountain climbing, ski-touring, snowshoeing, bicycling, camping, kayaking and canoeing, nature study, sailing, and adventure travel. The club's conservation division supports environmental causes through educational activities, sponsoring legislation, and presenting informational programs. All club activities are led by skilled, experienced volunteers, who are dedicated to promoting safe and responsible enjoyment and preservation of the outdoors.

If you would like to participate in these organized outdoor activities or the club's programs, consider a membership in The Mountaineers. For information and an application, write or call The Mountaineers, Club Headquarters, 300 Third Avenue West, Seattle, Washington 98119; (206) 284-6310.

The Mountaineers Books, an active, nonprofit publishing program of the club, produces guidebooks, instructional texts, historical works, natural history guides, and works on environmental conservation. All books produced by The Mountaineers are aimed at fulfilling the club's mission.

Send or call for our catalog of more than 300 outdoor titles:

 **The Mountaineers Books
1001 SW Klickitat Way, Suite 201
Seattle, WA 98134
1-800-553-4453**
**e-mail: mbooks@mountaineers.org
website: www.mountaineers.org**